CHEAP EATS

Budget-Busting Ideas That Won't Break the Bank

STERLING EPICURE
New York

STERLING EPICURE
New York

An Imprint of Sterling Publishing
387 Park Avenue South
New York, NY 10016

STERLING EPICURE is a trademark of Sterling Publishing Co., Inc.
The distinctive Sterling logo is a registered trademark of Sterling Publishing Co., Inc.

First published in the United Kingdom in 2013 by Pavilion Books Company Limited

ISBN 978-1-4549-1522-5

For information about custom editions, special sales, and premium and corporate purchases, please contact Sterling Special Sales at 800-805-5489 or specialsales@sterlingpublishing.com.

Manufactured in China

10 9 8 7 6 5 4 3 2 1

www.sterlingpublishing.com

NOTES
All spoon measures are level.

Ovens and broilers must be preheated to the specified temperature.

Large eggs should be used except where otherwise specified. Free-range eggs are recommended.

All-purpose, bread, self-rising, and wholewheat flours should unsifted and spooned into the cup measure and then leveled.

Note that some recipes contain raw or lightly cooked eggs. The young, elderly, pregnant women and anyone with an immune-deficiency disease should avoid these because of the slight risk of salmonella.

Contents

Bites and Sides for Loose Change

Keep It Seasonal

Why? Because not only will the produce you buy taste fantastic, it will also cost less. Look out for good deals at supermarkets, farm stands, markets, and farmer's markets, where you can sometimes buy larger, cheaper quantities for freezing or batch cooking. Pick Your Own farms often charge half the price of the supermarkets. You can pick fruit and vegetables at their ripest and enjoy a fun day out with the family, too.

January
Vegetables Beets, Brussels sprouts, cauliflower, celery root, celery, endive, Jerusalem artichokes, kale, leeks, parsnips, potatoes, rutabagas, turnips
Fruit Apples, clementines, kiwi, lemons, oranges, passion fruit, pears, pineapple, pomegranate, satsumas, tangerines, walnuts
Fish Clams, cockles, haddock, hake, lemon sole, mussels, flounder

February
Vegetables Brussels sprouts, cauliflower, celery root, endive, kale, leeks, parsnips, potatoes, rutabagas
Fruit Bananas, blood oranges, kiwi, lemons, oranges, passion fruit, pears, pineapple, pomegranate
Fish Cockles, cod, haddock, hake, lemon sole, mussels, salmon

March

Vegetables Cauliflower, endive, kale, leeks, purple sprouting broccoli, rhubarb, scallions

Fruit Bananas, blood oranges, kiwi, lemons, oranges, passion fruit, pineapple, pomegranate

Fish Cockles, cod, hake, lemon sole, mussels, salmon, sea trout

April

Vegetables Arugula, asparagus, broccoli, new potatoes, purple sprouting broccoli, radishes, rhubarb, spinach, scallions, watercress

Fruit Bananas, kiwi

Fish Cockles, cod, salmon, sea trout

May

Vegetables Arugula, asparagus, broccoli, new potatoes, radishes, rhubarb, spinach, scallions, watercress

Fruit Cherries, kiwi, strawberries

Meat Lamb

Fish Cod, crab, flounder, lemon sole, salmon, sea bass, sea trout

June

Vegetables Arugula, artichokes, asparagus, broccoli, carrots, eggplant, fava beans, fennel, new potatoes, peas, radishes, runner beans, scallions, snow peas, summer squash, turnips, watercress

Fruit Cherries, strawberries

Meat Lamb

Fish Cod, crab, flounder, haddock, herring, lemon sole, mackerel, salmon, sardines, sea bass, sea trout

July

Vegetables Arugula, artichokes, beets, broccoli, carrots, eggplant, fava beans, cucumber, fennel, garlic, green beans, snow peas, new potatoes, onions, peas, potatoes, radishes, runner beans, summer squash, turnips, watercress

Fruit Apricots, blackberries, blueberries, cherries, gooseberries, greengage plums, kiwi, melons, peaches, raspberries, red currants, strawberries, tomatoes

Meat Lamb, rabbit

Fish Cod, crab, flounder, haddock, herring, lemon sole, mackerel, salmon, sardines, sea bass, sea trout

August

Vegetables Arugula, artichokes, beets, broccoli, carrots, cucumber, eggplant, fennel, garlic, green beans, leeks, lima beans, snow peas, onions, peas, peppers, potatoes, radishes, runner beans, summer squash, sweet corn, watercress

Fruit Apricots, blackberries, blueberries, damson plums, greengage plums, kiwi, melons, nectarines, peaches, plums, raspberries, red currants, tomatoes

Meat Lamb, rabbit

Fish Cod, crab, flounder, haddock, herring, lemon sole, mackerel, mullet, salmon, sardines, sea bass

September

Vegetables Arugula, artichokes, beets, broccoli, butternut squash, carrots, cucumber, eggplant, fennel, garlic, leeks, onions, parsnips, peas, peppers, potatoes, radishes, runner beans, snow peas, summer squash, sweet corn, watercress, wild mushrooms

Fruit Apples, blackberries, damson plums, figs, grapes, melons, nectarines, peaches, pears, plums, raspberries, red currants, tomatoes, walnuts

Meat Lamb, rabbit

Fish Clams, cod, crab, flounder, haddock, herring, lemon sole, mackerel, mullet, sea bass, squid

October

Vegetables Artichokes, beets, broccoli, butternut squash, carrots, celery, celery root, fennel, kale, leeks, onions, parsnips, potatoes, pumpkin, rutabagas, turnips, watercress, wild mushrooms

Fruit Apples, chestnuts, figs, pears, quince, tomatoes, walnuts

Meat Rabbit

Fish Clams, crab, flounder, mullet, haddock, hake, lemon sole, mackerel, mussels, sea bass, squid

November

Vegetables Artichokes, beets, Brussels sprouts, celery, celery root, endive, kale, leeks, parsnips, potatoes, pumpkin, rutabagas, turnips, watercress, wild mushrooms

Fruit Apples, chestnuts, clementines, cranberries, figs, passion fruit, pears, quince, satsumas, tangerines, walnuts

Meat Rabbit

Fish Clams, haddock, hake, flounder, lemon sole, mussels, sea bass, squid

December

Vegetables Beets, Brussels sprouts, cauliflower, celery, celery root, endive, kale, leeks, parsnips, potatoes, pumpkin, rutabagas, turnips

Fruit Apples, chestnuts, clementines, cranberries, passion fruit, pears, pineapple, pomegranate, satsumas, tangerines, walnuts

Meat Rabbit

Fish Clams, flounder, haddock, hake, lemon sole, mussels, sea bass

Spanish Omelet

Prep time: 15 minutes
Cooking time: about 35 minutes

2lb. (900g) potatoes, peeled

3–4 tbsp. vegetable oil

1 onion, finely sliced

8 eggs

3 tbsp. freshly chopped flat-leaf parsley

3 bacon slices

salt and freshly ground black pepper

green salad to serve

1 Put the whole potatoes into a pot of cold salted water and bring to a boil, then reduce the heat and simmer for 15–20 minutes until almost cooked. When the potatoes are cool enough to handle, slice them thickly.

2 Heat 1 tbsp. of the oil in an 7in. (18cm) nonstick skillet (suitable for use under the broiler). Add the onion and fry gently for 7–10 minutes until softened. Remove from the heat and set aside.

3 Lightly beat the eggs in a bowl and season well with salt and ground black pepper.

4 Heat the broiler. Heat the remaining oil in the skillet, then layer the potato slices, onion, and 2 tbsp. of the chopped parsley in the pan. Pour in the beaten eggs and cook for 5–10 minutes until the omelet is firm underneath. Meanwhile, broil the bacon until crisp, then break into pieces.

5 Put the omelet in its pan under the broiler for 2–3 minutes until the top is just set. Scatter the bacon and remaining chopped parsley over the surface. Serve wedges of the omelet with a green salad.

Welsh Rarebit

Prep time: 10 minutes
Cooking time: about 15 minutes

1 can (15-oz./425g) crushed tomatoes

½ tbsp. tomato puree

1 small shallot, thinly sliced

1½ cups grated sharp cheddar cheese

½ tsp. dry English mustard

4 tbsp. ale or beer

a few dashes of Worcestershire sauce

1 extra-large egg yolk

1½ tbsp. finely chopped fresh parsley

8 crumpets or English muffins

salt and freshly ground black pepper

crisp green salad to serve

1 Put the tomatoes, tomato puree, and shallot into a small pot. Bring to a boil, reduce the heat and simmer for 10 minutes. Season with salt and black pepper.

2 Meanwhile, mix the cheese, mustard, ale, Worcestershire sauce, egg yolk, parsley, and salt and pepper together in a bowl.

3 Heat the broiler to medium. Arrange the crumpets on a cookie sheet and toast until golden. Spread the tomato sauce equally over the toasted crumpets, then top each with an equal amount of the cheese mixture. Broil for 3–5 minutes until bubbling and golden. Serve with a crisp green salad.

SAVE TIME

Make the tomato sauce mixture up to a day ahead. Cool, cover, and chill. When ready to serve, reheat gently and finish the recipe.

Serves 4

Make Your Own Soup

Soups are nutritious, full of flavor, and easy to make. Incredibly versatile, they can be smooth or chunky, light for a first course or substantial for a main course, made with vegetables, beans, meat, chicken, or fish.

You can use almost any mixture of vegetables.
To serve four, you will need:
2 tbsp. oil (or 1 tbsp. oil and 2 tbsp. butter), 1 or 2 finely chopped onions, 1 or 2 crushed garlic cloves, 3 cups chopped mixed vegetables, such as celery, fennel, leeks, potatoes, canned tomatoes, and parsnips (finely diced or larger dice for a chunky soup), and 4½ cups (1.1 liters) stock.

1 Fry the onions in the oil (or oil and butter) until soft, then add the garlic, if you like.
2 Add the mixed vegetables and the stock. Bring to a boil, then reduce the heat, and simmer for 20–30 minutes until the vegetables are tender.
3 Leave chunky, partially puree or blend until smooth.

Pureeing soups

1 **Using a blender** Leave the soup to cool slightly, then fill the jug about half-full, making sure that there is more liquid than solids. Cover the lid with a dish towel and hold it on tightly. Blend until smooth, then add more solids and blend again until all the soup is smooth. (If you have a lot of soup, transfer each batch to a clean pan.)

1

2   **Using a stick blender** Leave the soup to cool slightly. Stick the blender deep into the pot, turn it on and move it around so all the soup is pureed.

Note: don't do this in a nonstick pan.

3   **Using a food mill** A food mill makes a fine puree, although it takes longer than using a blender. Fit the fine plate in the food mill and set it over a bowl—put a dish towel underneath to keep it from moving on the counter. Fill the bowl of the food mill about halfway up the side, putting in more solids than liquid. Work in batches if you have a large quantity of soup.

4   **Using a sieve** If you don't have a blender or food mill, you can puree soup by pushing it through a sieve, although this takes a much longer time—and more work!

Partially pureed soups

1   For an interesting texture, puree one-third to half of the ingredients, then stir back into the soup.

2   Alternatively, prepare the vegetables or other ingredients, but keep a few choice pieces to one side. While the soup is cooking, steam or boil the reserved pieces until just tender; refresh green vegetables in cold water to set the color. Just before serving, cut into smaller pieces and add to the soup.

Chunky soups

1   Cut the ingredients into bite-size pieces. Heat the oil or oil and butter in the soup pot and cook the onions—and garlic if you like—until soft and lightly colored.

2   Add the remaining ingredients, putting in those that need the longest cooking first. Pour in some stock and bring to a boil.

3   Reduce the heat and simmer gently until all the ingredients are tender. If too much liquid boils away, simply add more.

Scotch Broth

Prep time: 15 minutes
Cooking time: about 1 hour

1 tbsp. vegetable oil

9oz. (250g) lamb neck tenderloin, cut into ¾in. (2cm) cubes

2 parsnips, roughly chopped

2 carrots, roughly chopped

1 onion, finely chopped

1 potato, finely diced

3 smoked bacon slices, thinly sliced

heaped 1 cup (125g) pearl barley

4¼ cups (1 liter) lamb or beef stock

½ cup frozen peas

salt and freshly ground black pepper

a small handful of fresh parsley, finely chopped, to garnish

1 Heat the oil over high heat in a large saucepan. Brown the lamb all over—do this in batches if necessary to keep the lamb from steaming rather than browning. Add the parsnips, carrots, onion, potato, and bacon and fry for 3–5 minutes.

2 Add the pearl barley and mix well. Pour in the stock and stir well, scraping any sticky goodness from the bottom of the pan. Bring to a boil, then reduce the heat, cover, and simmer gently for 40–50 minutes until the lamb is tender.

3 Stir in the peas and cook until warmed through, then season to taste with salt and pepper. Transfer to individual bowls, garnish the broth with parsley, and serve.

SAVE MONEY

Neck is an ideal cut of lamb to use when you are watching the pennies, and pearl barley adds great texture and body.

Serves 4

Spiced Cauliflower Soup

Prep time: 15 minutes
Cooking time: 35 minutes

1 tbsp. chili oil, plus extra to drizzle

1 onion, chopped

1 garlic clove, crushed

2 tsp. ground coriander

1 cauliflower, cut into florets

1 large potato, peeled and cubed

1 lemon

5¾ cups (1¼ quarts) chicken stock, hot

salt and freshly ground black pepper

2 tsp. extra virgin olive oil

6 tsp. plain yogurt

2 tbsp. slivered almonds, toasted,
    to garnish

SAVE TIME

Prepare the soup to the end of
step 2, then chill for up to two days.
Complete the recipe to serve.

1 Heat the chili oil in a large pan and gently fry the onion for 10 minutes, or until softened. Add a little salt to the pan now—this gives extra depth of flavor to the soup. Add the garlic and coriander and fry for 2 minutes. Stir in the cauliflower and potato and gently stir for 3 minutes.

2 Zest the lemon and add the zest to the pan with the hot stock. Season with salt and pepper and bring to a boil, then reduce the heat, cover, and simmer for 15–20 minutes until the vegetables are tender. Cool slightly. Working in batches, puree the soup in a blender until smooth.

3 Pour the soup back into the cleaned pan. Reheat gently and check the seasoning. Divide among six warm bowls.

4 Juice half the lemon and mix with the olive oil. Swirl 1 tsp. yogurt into each bowl. Drizzle with lemon oil and some extra chili oil, if you like, then garnish with the almonds. Serve immediately.

Serves 6

The Well-Stocked Refrigerator and Freezer

Using your appliances will make life so much easier in the kitchen. Consider the space you have available: do you have room for a separate refrigerator and freezer? Choose wisely to make sure you get the most out of what you can fit in your kitchen.

The perfect refrigerator

A refrigerator is vital for any kitchen and keeps food fresh for longer. It is, however, the main culprit for waste. The bigger it is, the more it becomes a repository for out-of-date condiments and bags of wilted salad greens that lurk in its depths.

Safe storage

- ❏ Cool cooked food to room temperature before putting it in the refrigerator
- ❏ Wrap or cover all food, except fruit and vegetables

- ❏ Practice refrigerator discipline: the coldest shelves are at the bottom, so store raw poultry, meat, and fish there
- ❏ Always separate cooked foods from raw foods

To make sure your refrigerator works properly:

- ❏ Don't overfill it
- ❏ Don't put hot foods in it
- ❏ Don't open the door more than necessary
- ❏ Clean it regularly

The perfect freezer

This is an invaluable tool and if you utilize it properly—particularly with batch cooking—you can save time and avoid waste. Make sure you leave enough time for food to thaw: if you leave it overnight in the refrigerator, your meal will be ready to pop into the oven when you get home from work. You can have all sorts of standbys waiting for you: breads, cakes, cookies, pastry, frozen vegetables, cream, stocks, soups, herbs, and meat, as well as fruit, such as raspberries and blackberries.

How to store food:

- ❑ Freeze food as soon as possible after purchase
- ❑ Label cooked food with the date and name of the dish
- ❑ Freeze food in portions
- ❑ Never put warm foods into the freezer; wait until they have cooled
- ❑ Check the manufacturer's instructions for freezing times
- ❑ Do not refreeze food once it has thawed

What not to store in the freezer:

- ❑ Whole eggs—freeze whites and yolks separately
- ❑ Fried foods—they lose their crispness and become soggy
- ❑ Vegetables, such as cucumber, lettuce, and celery that have too high a water content
- ❑ Some sauces—mayonnaise and similar sauces will separate when thawed

To make sure the freezer works properly:

- ❑ Defrost it regularly
- ❑ Keep the freezer as full as possible

Thawing and reheating food:

Each recipe will give you specific directions, but generally:

- ❑ Some foods, such as vegetables, soups, and sauces, can be cooked from frozen—dropped into boiling water, or heated until thawed
- ❑ Make sure other foods are thoroughly thawed before cooking
- ❑ Cook food as soon as possible after thawing
- ❑ Ensure food is piping hot all the way through after cooking

Anchovy Pizza Tart

Prep time: 20 minutes, plus rising
Cooking time: about 40 minutes

1⅔ cups bread flour, plus extra to dust

½ tsp. instant dry yeast

½ tsp. sugar

¼ tsp. salt

2 large onions, thinly sliced

½ cup vegetable oil

12 anchovies, marinated in oil, halved
lengthwise

15 cherry tomatoes, halved

1 tbsp. snipped fresh chives

green salad to serve

1 Sift the flour into a large bowl and mix
in the yeast, sugar, and salt. Quickly
stir in ⅔ cup (150ml) tepid water to
make a soft but not sticky dough.
Transfer to a lightly floured work
surface and knead for 3 minutes. Put
back into the bowl, cover with plastic
wrap, and let rise in a warm place for
20 minutes.

2 Meanwhile, put the onions into a pan
and pour the oil over them. Fry gently
for 15 minutes, or until soft. Strain,
reserving the oil.

3 Heat the oven to 400°F (350°F for
convection ovens). Lightly dust
a work surface with flour and roll out
the dough into a 12 × 12in. (30 × 30cm)
square. Transfer to a nonstick cookie
sheet. Brush with some of the reserved
onion oil, then spread the onions over.
Use the anchovy strips to make
a diagonal crisscross pattern on top
of the onions. Put a tomato half, cut
side up, in the middle of each diamond.
Bake for 20–25 minutes until golden.
Scatter with chives and serve in slices
with a green salad.

Serves 4

Iberian Potatoes

Prep time: 15 minutes
Cooking time: about 1½ hours

2 tbsp. olive oil

2 onions, thinly sliced

2 garlic cloves, thinly sliced

3 baking potatoes, thinly sliced

4 tomatoes, sliced

1 tsp. dried oregano

salt and freshly ground black pepper

2 cups (500ml) vegetable stock

1 Heat the oven to 400°F (350°F for convection ovens). Heat the oil in a large Dutch oven and gently fry the onions for 10 minutes, or until softened. Add the garlic and cook for 1 minute. Take the pot off the heat and use a slotted spoon to lift out the onion mixture and set aside.

2 Put half of the potato slices into the bottom of the pot, then top with the onion mixture, followed by the tomato slices. Sprinkle with the oregano and season well with salt and pepper. Top with a layer of the remaining potato slices, then pour the stock over.

3 Cover tightly and bake for 1¼ hours, removing the lid for the final 30–40 minutes so the potatoes brown. Serve as a side dish.

Serves 4

Braised Red Cabbage and Beet

Prep time: 15 minutes
Cooking time: about 2¼ hours

1 tbsp. olive oil

1 onion, finely chopped

1 garlic clove, crushed

2 tbsp. dark brown sugar

1 red cabbage, cored and shredded

1 beet, peeled and cut into chunks

leaves from a large fresh thyme sprig

2 tbsp. balsamic vinegar

1 tbsp. chopped fresh curly parsley

1 Heat the oven to 325°F (300°F for convection ovens). Heat the oil in a medium Dutch oven and gently fry the onion for 10 minutes, or until softened. Add the garlic and sugar and fry for 2 minutes.

2 Stir in the cabbage, beet, thyme, vinegar and 7 tbsp. water. Cover tightly and bake, stirring occasionally, for 2 hours, or until tender. Garnish with parsley to serve.

SAVE TIME

This is one of those recipes that tastes even better if you cook it in advance to give the ingredients time to mingle. Complete the recipe, but don't add the parsley garnish. Leave to cool and chill for up to two days. Reheat gently over low heat until piping hot, garnish, and serve.

Serves 6

Lemon Vinaigrette

To make about ⅔ cup (150ml), you will need:

2 tbsp. lemon juice, 2 tsp. honey, salt and freshly ground black pepper, ½ cup (125ml) extra virgin olive oil, 3 tbsp. chopped fresh mint, 4 tbsp. roughly chopped fresh parsley.

1 Put the lemon juice, honey, and salt and black pepper to taste into a small bowl and whisk together. Gradually whisk in the oil and stir in the herbs.
2 If not using immediately, store in a cool place and whisk briefly before using.

Lemon and Parsley

To make about ½ cup (125ml), you will need:

juice of ½ lemon, 6 tbsp. extra virgin olive oil, 4 tbsp. chopped fresh flat-leaf parsley, salt and freshly ground black pepper.

1 Put the lemon juice, oil, and parsley into a small bowl and whisk to combine. Season to taste with salt and black pepper.
2 If not using immediately, store in a cool place and whisk briefly before using.

Mustard

To make about ½ cup (125ml), you will need:

1 tbsp. wholegrain mustard, juice of ½ lemon, 6 tbsp. extra virgin olive oil, salt and freshly ground black pepper.

1 Put the mustard, lemon juice, and oil into a small bowl and whisk to combine. Season to taste with salt and black pepper.
2 If not using immediately, store in a cool place and whisk briefly before using.

Blue Cheese

To make about ½ cup (125ml), you will need:

2oz. (50g) Roquefort cheese, 2 tbsp. low-fat plain yogurt, 1 tbsp. white wine vinegar, 5 tbsp. extra virgin olive oil, salt and freshly ground black pepper.

1 Crumble the cheese into a food processor and add the yogurt, vinegar and oil. Blend for 1 minute until thoroughly combined. Season with salt and black pepper.

2 Store in a cool place and use within one day.

Chili Lime

To make about ½ cup (125ml), you will need:

¼ seeded and finely chopped red chili pepper (see Safety Tip, page 34), 1 crushed garlic clove, ½in. (1cm) peeled and finely grated piece of fresh ginger, juice of 1½ large limes, 4 tbsp. olive oil, 1½ tbsp. light brown sugar, 2 tbsp. fresh cilantro leaves, 2 tbsp. fresh mint leaves.

1 Put the chili pepper, garlic, ginger, lime juice, oil, and sugar into a food processor or blender and blend for 10 seconds to combine.
2 Add the cilantro and mint and blend together for 5 seconds to chop roughly.
3 Store in a cool place and use within two days.

Endive with Ham and Cheese

TAKE 5

🍴 **Prep time:** 5 minutes
Cooking time: about 10 minutes

---

4 large Belgian endive heads, halved
   lengthwise

8 slices of honey-roasted ham

8 slices of Gouda cheese

¼ cup fine fresh wholewheat
   bread crumbs

crusty bread and a mixed green salad
   to serve

---

1 Bring a large pot of water to a boil.
   Add the endive, reduce the heat and
   simmer for 3–5 minutes until just
   tender. Drain well.

2 Heat the broiler to medium. Wrap
   each cooked endive half in a slice
   of ham, then arrange, cut side down,
   on a baking sheet. Lay a slice
   of cheese over each endive half and
   top with some of the bread crumbs.
   Broil for 3–5 minutes until piping hot
   and golden. Serve with crusty bread
   and a mixed green salad.

Serves 4

Warm Smoked Salmon and Cucumber Salad

Prep time: 10 minutes
Cooking time: about 5 minutes

½ tbsp. vegetable oil

1in. (2.5cm) piece of fresh ginger, peeled and finely chopped

1 green chili pepper, seeded and finely chopped (see Safety Tip)

1 tbsp. sesame seeds

6 baby corn cobs, thinly sliced

11oz. (300g) instant rice noodles

1 cucumber, peeled into ribbons

1 tbsp. toasted sesame oil

1 tbsp. soy sauce

4oz. (125g) smoked salmon trimmings

salt and freshly ground black pepper

a large handful of fresh cilantro, finely chopped, to garnish

lime wedges to serve

1 Heat the vegetable oil in a large skillet or wok. Add the ginger, chili, and sesame seeds and cook for 1 minute. Stir in the baby corn and noodles and cook, stirring frequently, for 3 minutes, or until the noodles are tender.

2 Add the cucumber, sesame oil, soy sauce, and salmon and heat through. Season to taste with salt and pepper. Garnish with cilantro and serve with lime wedges.

SAFETY TIP

Chili peppers can be very mild to blisteringly hot, depending on the type of chili and its ripeness. Taste a small piece first to make sure it's not too hot for you. Be extremely careful when handling chilies not to touch or rub your eyes with your fingers, or they will sting. Wash knives immediately after cutting chilies. As a precaution, use rubber gloves when preparing them, if you like.

Serves 4

Simple Fried Rice

TAKE
5

Prep time: 5 minutes
Cooking time: about 20 minutes

¾ cup long-grain rice

2 tbsp. sesame oil

3 eggs, lightly beaten

1¾ cups frozen baby peas

9oz. (250g) cooked shelled shrimp

1 Cook the rice in boiling water for about 10 minutes, or according to the package directions. Drain well.

2 Heat 1 tsp. of the sesame oil in a large, nonstick skillet. Pour in half the beaten eggs and tilt the pan around over the heat for about 1 minute until the egg is set. Transfer the omelet to a warm plate. Repeat with another 1 tsp. sesame oil and the remaining beaten egg to make another omelet. Transfer to another warm plate.

3 Add the remaining oil to the pan and stir in the rice and peas. Stir-fry for 2–3 minutes until the peas are cooked. Stir in the shrimp.

4 Roll up the omelets and roughly chop one-third of one, then slice the remainder into strips. Add the chopped omelet to the rice, peas, and shrimp and cook for 1–2 minutes until heated through. Divide the fried rice among four serving bowls, top with the sliced omelets, and serve immediately.

Serves 4

Sardines on Toast

Prep time: 5 minutes
Cooking time: about 10 minutes

4 thick slices wholegrain bread

2 large tomatoes, sliced

2 cans (3¾-oz./120g) sardines in olive oil, drained

juice of ½ lemon

a small handful of fresh flat-leaf parsley, chopped

1 Heat the broiler. Toast the slices of bread on both sides.

2 Divide the tomato slices and the sardines between the toast slices and squeeze the lemon juice over them. Put back under the broiler for 2–3 minutes to heat through. Scatter the parsley over the sardines and serve immediately.

TRY THIS

An easy way to get a brand new dish is to use a can of sardines in tomato sauce instead of the sardines in oil.

Serves 4

Frugal Family Suppers

Midweek Meal Planner

Squash Risotto with Hazelnut Butter

Warm Salmon and Potato Salad

Quick Creamy Gnocchi

Spicy Baked Eggs

Ham, Leek, and Mushroom Fusilli

Cheese and Chicken Potato Cakes

Orange and Ginger Beef Stir-Fry

Creamy Cider Chicken

Cherry Tomato and Goat Cheese Tart

Stuffed Chicken Thighs

Lamb, Lentil, and Chili Soup

Barbecue Minute Steak Sandwiches

Chicken and Squash Gratin

Mustard Lamb Chops

Spicy Pork Meatballs

Bean and Bacon Stew

Beef Pilaf

Crispy-Crumbed Cabbage Linguine

Jarlsberg and Sweet Onion Tart

Smoked Haddock and Spinach Frittata

Squash Risotto with Hazelnut Butter

Prep time: 20 minutes
Cooking time: about 50 minutes

1 tbsp. vegetable oil

3½ cups peeled butternut squash cut into ¾in. (2cm) cubes

1 onion, finely chopped

1 garlic clove, finely chopped

1½ cups risotto rice, such as Arborio or carnaroli

¼ cup dry white wine

4½ cups (1.1 liters) vegetable stock, hot

salt and freshly ground black pepper

2 tbsp. butter

⅓ cup blanched hazelnuts, chopped

4 fresh sage leaves, thinly sliced

1 Heat half the oil in a large pan over medium heat. Fry the squash, tossing occasionally, for 15–20 minutes until tender. Lift the squash out of the pan and transfer to a plate.

2 Add the remaining oil to the pan and gently fry the onion for 10 minutes, or until tender. Stir in the garlic and rice and cook for 2 minutes, or until the rice is translucent. Stir in the wine and let boil, stirring frequently, until the liquid has evaporated.

3 Gradually add the hot stock, one ladleful at a time, adding another ladleful only when the previous one has been absorbed. Stir well after each addition. Continue until the rice is almost fully cooked—this will take about 15 minutes.

4 Gently stir the cooked squash into the risotto and reheat. Season to taste with salt and pepper, then cover the pan and set aside.

5 Heat the butter and hazelnuts together in a small skillet until the butter is light brown and the nuts are lightly toasted, then add the sage. Divide the risotto among four warm bowls, garnish with the hazelnut butter and serve.

TRY THIS

Use a few pinches of dried sage if you don't have any fresh.

Serves 4

Warm Salmon and Potato Salad

Prep time: 15 minutes
Cooking time: about 50 minutes

1lb. 11oz. (750g) new potatoes, quartered

1 red onion, cut into wedges

1 tbsp. olive oil

7oz. (200g) cherry tomatoes

4 × 5oz. (150g) salmon fillets

salt and freshly ground black pepper

1 bag (10oz./280g) of watercress

fresh basil leaves to garnish (optional)

For the dressing

juice of 1 lemon

1 tbsp. wholegrain mustard

1 tbsp. honey

¼ cup olive oil

1 Heat the oven to 425°F (400°F for convection ovens). Put the potatoes and onion wedges into a medium roasting pan, add the oil, and stir to coat. Spread the vegetables out and roast for 35 minutes, or until just tender.

2 Remove the pan from the oven, stir in the cherry tomatoes, and lay the salmon fillets on top of the vegetables. Season well with salt and pepper and put back into the oven for 12 minutes longer, or until the fish is opaque and cooked through.

3 Meanwhile, in a small bowl, whisk together the lemon juice, mustard, honey, oil, a splash of water, and plenty of salt and pepper until combined.

4 Arrange the watercress on a large platter or divide among four warm plates. Carefully slide the cooked vegetables and salmon on top of the watercress. Pour the dressing over and garnish with basil, if you like.

Serves 4

Cherry Tomato and Goat Cheese Tart

Prep time: 10 minutes
Cooking time: about 25 minutes

11½oz. (325g) bought puff pastry dough (in a rectangular sheet), fresh or thawed

4oz. (125g) soft goat cheese

1 tsp. sugar

2¼ cups halved cherry tomatoes

salt and freshly ground black pepper

1 tbsp. balsamic vinegar

1 tbsp. extra virgin olive oil

a small handful of fresh basil leaves, torn, to garnish

green salad to serve

1 Heat the oven to 425°F (400°F for convection ovens). Line a cookie sheet with parchment paper.

2 Unroll the pastry dough sheet onto the prepared cookie sheet. Crumble or spread the cheese over the dough, leaving a ½in. (1cm) border around the edges. Sprinkle half the sugar over the cheese, then arrange the tomatoes on top, cut side up. Season well with salt and pepper, then sprinkle the remaining sugar over the top.

3 Bake the tart for 25 minutes, or until the pastry is golden and puffed. Take out of the oven and drizzle with the vinegar and oil, then garnish with torn basil leaves. Serve warm or at room temperature with a green salad.

Stuffed Chicken Thighs

Prep time: 20 minutes
Cooking time: about 30 minutes

2 cups fresh white bread crumbs

3 tbsp. freshly grated Parmesan cheese

2 eggs, lightly beaten

3 tbsp. chopped fresh basil

finely grated zest of 1 lemon

salt and freshly ground black pepper

8 boneless, skinless chicken thighs

8 slices of smoked bacon

seasonal vegetables to serve

TRY THIS

Use 1 tbsp. dried basil if you don't
have any fresh.

1 Heat the oven to 425°F (400°F for convection ovens). Put the bread crumbs, cheese, eggs, basil, lemon zest, and plenty of salt and pepper into a medium bowl and stir to combine.

2 Open out the chicken thighs on a cutting board, skinned side down. Spoon some of the mixture down the middle of each, then fold the meat over the filling. Wrap a slice of bacon around each thigh to help secure the filling in place.

3 Transfer the stuffed thighs, seam side down, to a nonstick baking sheet and roast for 25–30 minutes until golden and cooked through. Serve with seasonal vegetables.

Serves 4

Lamb, Lentil, and Chili Soup

Prep time: 15 minutes
Cooking time: about 1 hour 40 minutes

1 tbsp. vegetable oil

12oz. (350g) lamb neck tenderloin, cut into small cubes

1 onion, finely chopped

2 carrots, finely chopped

1 celery rib, finely chopped

1 tsp. ground cumin

1 tsp. ground coriander

1½ cups yellow split peas

5¾ pints (1¼ quarts) vegetable stock

1 bay leaf

salt and freshly ground black pepper

To serve

2 tbsp. plain yogurt

1 red chili pepper, seeded and sliced into rings (see Safety Tip, page 34)

a small handful of fresh flat-leaf parsley or cilantro leaves, roughly chopped

crusty bread to serve

1 Heat the oil in a large pot over medium heat and fry the lamb until nicely browned. (Do this in batches if necessary to keep the meat from steaming.) Lift the lamb out of the pot and set aside, leaving as much oil in the pan as possible.

2 Add the chopped vegetables to the pot and cook for 5 minutes, or until softened. Stir in the spices and fry for 2 minutes longer. Put the lamb back into the pot with the split peas, stock, and bay leaf. Bring to a boil, then reduce the heat, cover, and simmer for about 1 hour 20 minutes, stirring and mashing it occasionally, until the lamb is tender and the mixture has cooked down to a fairly smooth soup.

3 Season to taste with salt and pepper and adjust the consistency if you like with more stock or water. Ladle into warm bowls. Garnish with a swirl of yogurt, some fresh chili, and herb leaves and serve with crusty bread.

Serves 4

Week 1 Shopping List

Chilled & Frozen

- ❑ 8 boneless, skinless chicken thighs
- ❑ 12oz. (350g) lamb neck tenderloin
- ❑ 8 smoked bacon slices
- ❑ 4 × 5oz. (150g) salmon fillets
- ❑ 4oz. (125g) soft goat cheese
- ❑ 2 eggs
- ❑ Parmesan cheese
- ❑ Butter
- ❑ Small pot plain yogurt
- ❑ 11½oz. (325g) puff pastry dough (in a rectangular sheet), fresh or frozen

Fruit, Vegetables, & Herbs

- ❑ 2 onions
- ❑ 1 red onion
- ❑ 1 head of garlic
- ❑ 1 red chili pepper
- ❑ 1lb. 11oz. (750g) new potatoes
- ❑ 1lb. 2oz. (500g) cherry tomatoes
- ❑ 2 carrots
- ❑ 1lb. 2oz. (500g) butternut squash
- ❑ 1 celery rib
- ❑ 2 lemons
- ❑ Fresh sage
- ❑ Large bunch fresh basil
- ❑ Fresh parsley or cilantro
- ❑ 3oz. (75g) watercress
- ❑ Mixed green salad leaves
- ❑ Extra seasonal vegetables, to serve

Pantry

(In case you need to restock)

- ❏ Vegetable oil
- ❏ Olive oil
- ❏ Extra virgin olive oil
- ❏ Vegetable stock
- ❏ Balsamic vinegar
- ❏ Wholegrain mustard
- ❏ Blanched hazelnuts
- ❏ Yellow split peas
- ❏ Honey
- ❏ Sugar
- ❏ Ground cumin
- ❏ Ground coriander
- ❏ 1 bay leaf
- ❏ Risotto rice, such as Arborio or carnaroli
- ❏ Few slices of white bread (for making bread crumbs)
- ❏ Dry white wine
- ❏ Crusty bread, to serve

Quick Creamy Gnocchi

Prep time: 10 minutes
Cooking time: about 15 minutes

2 tbsp. olive oil

1½lb. (700g) fresh gnocchi

7oz. (200g) cream cheese

1½ cups frozen peas

finely grated zest of ½ lemon

2 tbsp. snipped fresh chives

7 tbsp.–about ¾ cup (100–200ml) milk,
  as needed

salt and freshly ground black pepper

¼ cup grated cheddar cheese

scant 1 cup fresh white bread crumbs

crisp green salad to serve

1 Heat the broiler. Heat the oil in a large, deep skillet over high heat and add the gnocchi. Fry, stirring occasionally, until the gnocchi are becoming golden and softening—about 10 minutes.

2 Stir in the cream cheese, peas, lemon zest, most of the chives, the milk, and salt and pepper to taste. (Start with 7 tbsp. milk and add more if you prefer a looser mixture.) Cook until heated through, then transfer to a flameproof serving dish and sprinkle the cheese, bread crumbs, and remaining chives over the top.

3 Broil until golden and bubbling. Serve immediately with a crisp green salad.

Serves 4

Spicy Baked Eggs

Prep time: 15 minutes
Cooking time: about 35 minutes

1 tbsp. oil

1 red onion, thinly sliced

1 red chili pepper, seeded and finely
chopped (see Safety Tip, page 34)

1 garlic clove, crushed

2 cans (15-oz/425g) cans crushed
tomatoes

1 tsp. sugar

1 can (15-oz./425g) can kidney beans,
drained and rinsed

a large handful of fresh cilantro, roughly
chopped, plus extra to garnish

8 eggs

salt and freshly ground black pepper

sour cream and crusty bread to serve

1 Heat the oven to 400°F (350°F for
convection ovens). Heat the oil
in a large skillet and gently cook the
onion for 10 minutes, or until softened.
Stir in the chili and garlic and cook for
1 minute longer.

2 Add the tomatoes, sugar, and kidney
beans and simmer for 5 minutes. Stir
in the cilantro and season with salt
and pepper.

3 Transfer to a large, shallow baking
dish suitable for serving from. Make
a small indentation in the mixture
and crack an egg into it. Repeat with
the remaining eggs, spacing them
apart evenly.

4 Bake the eggs for 15–20 minutes
until the whites are set. Garnish with
cilantro and serve with sour cream
and some crusty bread.

Barbecue Minute Steak Sandwiches

Prep time: 15 minutes
Cooking time: about 2 minutes

4 tbsp. butter, softened

1½ tbsp. barbecue sauce

1 tbsp. wholegrain mustard

4 slices country-style bread

1 tbsp. olive oil

4 × minute/thin frying steaks

a large handful of arugula

3 tomatoes, sliced

1 Mix the butter, barbecue sauce, and mustard together and set aside. Toast the bread.

2 Meanwhile, heat the oil in a large skillet over high heat. When the pan is hot, add the steaks and cook for about 20 seconds on each side, depending on your preference.

3 Pile some arugula and tomato slices onto each piece of toast, then put a steak on top. Add a dollop of the barbecue butter and serve.

Serves 4

Chicken and Squash Gratin

Prep time: 15 minutes
Cooking time: about 50 minutes

1 tbsp. vegetable oil

1 onion, thinly sliced

1 leek, thickly sliced

3¼ cups peeled butternut squash cut into 1in. (2.5cm) pieces

3 boneless, skinless chicken breast halves, cut into bite-size strips

4 tbsp. butter

scant ½ cup all-purpose flour

2 cups (500ml) milk

7 tbsp. mascarpone cheese

2 tsp. dried tarragon

salt and freshly ground black pepper

1 cup ciabatta bread torn into small pieces

green salad to serve

1 Heat the oil in a large saucepan and gently cook the onion, leek, and squash for 15 minutes, stirring occasionally, or until softened. Set aside.

2 Meanwhile, put the chicken into a separate pan, cover with cold water, and bring to a boil. Reduce the heat and simmer for 5 minutes. Drain and add to the pan of vegetables.

3 Heat the oven to 350°F (325°F for convection ovens). Melt the butter in the empty pan, stir in the flour, and cook for 1 minute. Remove from the heat and gradually whisk in the milk to make a smooth sauce. Return to the heat and cook, stirring, until thickened. Stir in the mascarpone and tarragon and season with salt and pepper. Stir the sauce into the chicken and vegetable pan.

4 Transfer the mixture to a baking dish suitable for serving from and top with the bread. Bake for about 30 minutes until the bread is golden and the filling is bubbling. Serve with a green salad.

Serves 4

Mustard Lamb Chops

Prep time: 10 minutes, plus marinating (optional)
Cooking time: about 15 minutes

3 tbsp. red currant jelly

1 tbsp. Dijon mustard

salt and freshly ground black pepper

8 lamb loin chops, excess fat trimmed

boiled or roasted new potatoes and
a mixed green salad to serve

For the sauce

3 tbsp. mayonnaise

3 tbsp. crème fraîche or sour cream

1 tsp. wholegrain mustard

1 Stir together the red currant jelly, mustard, and salt and pepper to taste in a nonmetallic bowl. Add the lamb chops and turn to make sure they are well coated. If you have time, marinate in the refrigerator for 1 hour.

2 Heat the broiler to medium. Arrange the chops on a nonstick baking sheet and broil for 15 minutes, turning occasionally, or until they are browned and cooked to your liking. (Watch them carefully, because the sugar in the jelly can make them burn a little faster than usual). Carefully remove the baking sheet from under the broiler and cover with foil. Leave the chops to rest while you make the sauce.

3 Put the mayonnaise, crème fraîche, and mustard into a small serving bowl and stir to combine. Serve the chops with the sauce, some boiled or roasted new potatoes and a green salad.

Serves 4

Week 2 Shopping List

Chilled & Frozen

- ☐ 4 × minute/thin frying steaks
- ☐ 3 boneless, skinless chicken breast halves
- ☐ 8 lamb loin chops
- ☐ 1½lb. (700g) fresh gnocchi
- ☐ 8 eggs
- ☐ Butter
- ☐ Milk
- ☐ 3½oz. (100g) mascarpone cheese
- ☐ 7oz. (200g) cream cheese
- ☐ Cheddar cheese
- ☐ Small tub crème fraîche or sour cream
- ☐ Frozen peas
- ☐ Sour cream, to serve

Fruit, Vegetables, & Herbs

- ☐ 1 onion
- ☐ 1 red onion
- ☐ 1 head of garlic
- ☐ 3 tomatoes
- ☐ 1 leek
- ☐ 1 butternut squash
- ☐ 1 red chili pepper
- ☐ Fresh chives
- ☐ Fresh cilantro
- ☐ Small bag arugula
- ☐ 1 lemon
- ☐ Mixed green salad leaves, to serve
- ☐ New potatoes, to serve

Pantry

(In case you need to restock)

- ❑ Vegetable oil
- ❑ Olive oil
- ❑ 2 cans (15-oz/425g) crushed tomatoes
- ❑ All-purpose flour
- ❑ 1 can (15-oz/425g) kidney beans
- ❑ Red currant jelly
- ❑ Barbecue sauce
- ❑ Wholegrain mustard
- ❑ Dijon mustard
- ❑ Mayonnaise
- ❑ Sugar
- ❑ Dried tarragon
- ❑ Few slices of white bread (for making bread crumbs)
- ❑ Country-style bread
- ❑ Ciabatta bread
- ❑ Crusty bread, to serve

Ham, Leek, and Mushroom Fusilli

Prep time: 10 minutes
Cooking time: about 15 minutes

3 cups dried fusilli pasta (or use a pasta shape of your choice)

1 tbsp. vegetable oil

1 leek, thinly sliced

1 garlic clove, finely chopped

4¼ cups halved button mushrooms

1½ cups chopped cooked ham

1¼ cups low-fat crème fraîche or sour cream

a large handful of arugula

salt and freshly ground black pepper

1 Bring a large pot of salted water to a boil and cook the pasta according to the package directions.

2 Meanwhile, heat the oil in a large, deep skillet and gently cook the leek for 5 minutes. Add the garlic and mushrooms and cook for 8 minutes longer, or until the vegetables are tender. Stir in the chopped ham and crème fraîche.

3 When the pasta is cooked to your liking, set aside one cupful of the cooking water before draining. Stir the pasta into the sauce, then add enough of the reserved pasta water to make a smooth consistency. Season well with salt and pepper, then add the arugula and fold gently to combine. Serve immediately.

Serves 4

e and Chicken Potato Cakes

Prep time: 20 minutes
Cooking time: about 35 minutes

⅔ cup frozen peas

2¼lb. (1kg) baking potatoes, such as Idaho

3 tbsp. all-purpose flour

1 egg, lightly beaten

4 scallions, thinly sliced

2 cooked boneless, skinless chicken breast halves, finely chopped

scant 1 cup grated cheddar cheese

2 tbsp. vegetable oil

salt and freshly ground black pepper

mixed green salad to serve

TRY THIS

These rösti-like bakes are great for using up leftover cooked meat and vegetables. Try adding some chopped cooked sausage or ham instead of the chicken.

1 Heat the oven to 400°F (350°F for convection ovens). Line a baking sheet with parchment paper. Fill a kettle and bring to a boil. Put the peas into a colander in the sink, then pour the boiling water over them and set aside.

2 Peel and coarsely grate the potatoes. Pile the grated potato onto a clean dish towel, gather up the corners and squeeze out as much moisture as you can. Empty the squeezed potato into a large bowl, then mix in the remaining ingredients and season well with salt and pepper. Form the mixture into eight patties and arrange on the prepared baking sheet.

3 Bake in the oven for 30–35 minutes until golden and cooked through. Serve with a mixed green salad.

Serves 4

y Pork Meatballs

Prep time: 15 minutes
Cooking time: about 35 minutes

For the meatballs

3 tbsp. olive oil

14oz. (400g) ground pork

½–1 red chili pepper, to taste, seeded and finely chopped (see Safety Tip, page 34)

½ tbsp. wholegrain mustard

½ onion, finely chopped

1 egg

1½ cups fresh white bread crumbs

salt and freshly ground black pepper

boiled rice to serve

For the sauce

1 tbsp. olive oil

½ onion, finely chopped

½ tsp. smoked or sweet paprika

7 tbsp. red wine or beef stock

2 cans (15-oz./425g) crushed tomatoes

fresh cilantro or parsley, roughly torn, to garnish (optional)

salt and freshly ground black pepper

1 Heat the oven to 400°F (350°F for convection ovens). For the meatballs, pour the oil onto a baking sheet and put into the oven to heat up.

2 Put the ground pork, chili, mustard, onion, egg, bread crumbs, and salt and pepper to taste into a large bowl. Use your hands to mix together gently, then roll into golf ball-size balls.

3 Carefully take the baking sheet out of the oven, add the meatballs, and carefully roll them to coat in the oil. Put the baking sheet back into the oven and bake for 25 minutes, turning the meatballs occasionally, or until golden and cooked through.

4 Meanwhile, make the sauce. Heat the oil in a large pan and gently cook the onion for 10 minutes, or until softened. Stir in the paprika and cook for 1 minute, then add the wine or stock and cook for 1 minute longer. Stir in

the tomatoes and simmer for
15 minutes, or until the sauce is
thick and pulpy. Season to taste
with salt and pepper.

5 Add the meatballs to the tomato
sauce and cook for 5 minutes longer.
Garnish with cilantro or parsley, if
you like, and serve with rice.

HEALTHY TIP

If you want to make these meatballs
healthier, use ground turkey instead
of pork.

Serves 4

Bean and Bacon Stew

Prep time: 15 minutes
Cooking time: about 50 minutes

1 tbsp. vegetable oil

7oz. (200g) smoked back bacon, cut into
¼in. (0.5cm) pieces

1 onion, chopped

2 red bell peppers, seeded and
roughly chopped

2 cans (15-oz./425g) crushed tomatoes

a large pinch of dried chili flakes

2 cans (15-oz./425g) cannellini beans,
drained and rinsed

a large handful of fresh cilantro,
roughly torn

salt and freshly ground black pepper

crusty bread to serve (optional)

1 Heat the oil in a large pan over medium heat and fry the bacon for 5–6 minutes until golden. Lift out and set aside, leaving the oil in the pan.

2 Add the onion, peppers, and a splash of water to the pan and cook for 10 minutes, or until softened. Stir in the cooked bacon, the tomatoes, chili flakes, and 1 cup water. Bring the mixture to a boil, then reduce the heat, cover, and simmer for 20 minutes, stirring occasionally.

3 Uncover the pan, add the beans and cook for 10 minutes longer. Stir in the cilantro and season with salt and pepper. Serve with crusty bread, if you like.

TRY THIS

This stew is also delicious using
cans of mixed beans.

Serves 4

Beef Pilaf

Prep time: 10 minutes
Cooking time: about 40 minutes

1 tbsp. vegetable oil

1 onion, thinly sliced

1lb. (450g) boneless stewing beef, cubed

2 tbsp. garam masala

1 cup basmati rice

2 cups (500ml) chicken stock

7oz. (200g) green beans, trimmed

½ cup chopped dried apricots

4 tbsp. mango chutney

salt and freshly ground black pepper

To garnish

2 tbsp. slivered almonds

freshly chopped parsley or cilantro
   (optional)

1 Heat the oil in a large pan, then fry the onion for 8 minutes, or until softened. Add the beef and fry for 10 minutes, or until browned. (Add a splash of water if the pan looks too dry.) Stir in the garam masala and rice and fry for 1 minute longer.

2 Pour in the chicken stock and bring to a boil, then reduce the heat, cover, and simmer for 10 minutes.

3 Stir in the beans and apricots, then cover again and cook for 10 minutes longer, or until the stock is absorbed and the rice is tender. Fold in the chutney and season to taste with salt and pepper. Garnish with slivered almonds and chopped parsley or cilantro, if you like.

TRY THIS

An easy way to get a brand new dish is to make this recipe with chopped lamb neck tenderloin.

Serves 4

Week 3 Shopping List

Chilled & Frozen

- [ ] 1lb. (450g) stewing beef, cubed
- [ ] 2 cooked boneless, skinless chicken breast halves
- [ ] 14oz. (400g) ground pork
- [ ] 7oz. (200g) smoked bacon
- [ ] 7oz. (200g) cooked ham
- [ ] 11oz. (300g) low-fat crème fraîche or sour cream
- [ ] 3½oz. (100g) cheddar cheese
- [ ] 2 eggs
- [ ] Frozen peas

Fruit, Vegetables, & Herbs

- [ ] 3 onions
- [ ] 1 head of garlic
- [ ] 2 red bell peppers
- [ ] 2¼lb. (1kg) baking potatoes, such as Idaho
- [ ] 11oz. (300g) button mushrooms
- [ ] 1 leek
- [ ] 7oz. (200g) green beans
- [ ] 1 red chili pepper
- [ ] 4 scallions
- [ ] Fresh cilantro
- [ ] Fresh parsley (optional)
- [ ] Bag of arugula
- [ ] Mixed green salad leaves, to serve

Pantry

(In case you need to restock)

- ☐ Vegetable oil
- ☐ Olive oil
- ☐ Chicken stock
- ☐ Red wine or beef stock
- ☐ All-purpose flour
- ☐ 4 cans (15-oz./425g) cans crushed tomatoes
- ☐ 2 cans (15-oz./425g) cannellini beans
- ☐ Mango chutney
- ☐ Wholegrain mustard
- ☐ 12oz. (350g) dried fusilli pasta
- ☐ Smoked or sweet paprika
- ☐ Dried chilli flakes
- ☐ Garam masala
- ☐ Slivered almonds
- ☐ Dried apricots
- ☐ Basmati rice
- ☐ Boiled rice, to serve
- ☐ Few slices of white bread (for making bread crumbs)
- ☐ Crusty bread, to serve (optional)

Orange and Ginger Beef Stir-Fry

Prep time: 15 minutes
Cooking time: about 8 minutes

1 tbsp. cornstarch

6 tbsp. orange juice, no pulp

2 tbsp. soy sauce

1 tbsp. vegetable oil

14oz. (400g) boneless tender beef, cut into strips

2in. (5cm) piece of fresh ginger, peeled and cut into matchsticks

2½ cups prepared mixed stir-fry vegetables of your choice, chopped if large

salt and freshly ground black pepper

1 tbsp. sesame seeds

cooked egg noodles to serve

1 Put the cornstarch into a small bowl and gradually whisk in the orange juice followed by the soy sauce to make a smooth mixture. Set aside.

2 Heat the oil over high heat in a large skillet or wok. Add the beef strips and stir-fry for 1–2 minutes. Stir in the ginger, vegetables, and a splash of water and stir-fry until the vegetables are just tender and the beef is cooked to your liking.

3 Add the orange juice mixture to the pan and cook, stirring occasionally, until thick and syrupy—about 30 seconds. Season to taste with salt and pepper and sprinkle with the sesame seeds. Serve immediately with egg noodles.

SAVE TIME

As with all stir-fries, have your ingredients prepared and ready to go before you start cooking.

Serves 4

...y Cider Chicken

Prep time: 10 minutes
Cooking time: about 30 minutes

1 tbsp. vegetable oil

4 boneless, skinless chicken breast halves

1 onion, thinly sliced

½ tbsp. all-purpose flour

⅔ cup (150ml) applejack or apple cider

⅔ cup (150ml) heavy cream

2 tbsp. wholegrain mustard

a small handful of fresh flat-leaf parsley, chopped

salt and freshly ground black pepper

boiled rice or crusty bread to serve

1 Heat the oil in a large pan over high heat and fry the chicken breasts for 5 minutes on each side, or until golden. Lift the chicken out of the pan and set aside. Add the onion to the pan and fry for 8 minutes, or until softened.

2 Stir in the flour until the onions are coated, then add the applejack, cream, and ¾ cup plus 2 tbsp. (200ml) water. Put the chicken back into the pan and simmer for 12–15 minutes until cooked through. (Cut into one piece to make sure the meat is completely opaque and the juices run clear.)

3 Stir in the mustard and parsley and season well with salt and pepper. Serve with boiled rice or crusty bread.

SAVE TIME

To speed up cooking time, slice the whole breasts of chicken into thin strips.

Crispy-Crumbed Cabbage Linguine

Prep time: 15 minutes
Cooking time: about 15 minutes

14oz. (400g) dried linguine or spaghetti

2 tbsp. extra virgin olive oil

1 cup fresh white bread crumbs

4¼ cups shredded Savoy cabbage

2 garlic cloves, crushed

1 can (2-oz./50g) anchovies in olive oil

finely grated zest of 1 lemon

a small handful of fresh parsley,
roughly chopped

salt and freshly ground black pepper

1 Bring a large pot of salted water to a boil and cook the pasta according to the package directions.

2 Meanwhile, heat 1 tbsp. of the oil in a large, deep skillet. Cook the bread crumbs, stirring frequently, until golden and crisp—about 5 minutes. Transfer to a plate and set aside.

3 Put the skillet back onto the heat and add the remaining oil. Stir in the cabbage and garlic and fry for 1 minute, then add two ladlefuls of pasta cooking water and cook until the cabbage is just tender. Add the anchovies with their oil and some ground black pepper, stirring to break up the fish. Set aside.

4 Drain the pasta well and put back into the empty pan. Add the lemon zest and the cabbage mixture and toss well, then season with salt and pepper. Divide the linguine among four bowls and sprinkle the fried crumbs and the parsley over. Serve immediately.

Jarlsberg and Sweet Onion Tart

Prep time: 20 minutes
Cooking time: about 1 hour

all-purpose flour for dusting

13oz. (375g) bought piecrust dough

1 tbsp. olive oil

2 large onions, thinly sliced

1 tsp. sugar

1 cup finely diced Jarlsberg cheese

3 eggs

¾ cup plus 2 tbsp. (200ml) heavy cream

2 tbsp. chopped fresh chives or parsley

salt and freshly ground black pepper

green salad to serve

1 Heat the oven to 400°F (350°F for convection ovens). Lightly dust a surface with flour and roll out the dough large enough to line an 8in. (20cm) round, 1½in. (4cm) deep, fluted tart pan. Prick all over with a fork.

2 Line the dough with a sheet of parchment paper and fill with pie weights or dried beans. Put the pan on a cookie sheet and bake for 15–20 minutes until the pastry sides are set.

3 While the pastry is baking, heat the oil in a large pan and gently cook the onions for 15–20 minutes, covered, until very soft. Stir in the sugar, turn up the heat, and cook, stirring frequently, until the onions are lightly caramelized. Set aside.

4 Carefully remove the parchment and pie weights from the tart pan and return the pastry to the oven. Bake for 10 minutes longer, or until the crust is baked through and feels sandy to the touch. Remove the pan from the oven and reduce the oven temperature to 350°F (300°F for convection ovens).

5 Spoon the onions on to the tart shell and top with the diced cheese. Put the eggs into a large measuring cup and beat lightly, then mix in the cream, herbs, and plenty of salt and pepper. Pour over the onions and bake for 25–30 minutes until set and lightly golden. Serve warm or at room temperature with a green salad.

Serves 4

Smoked Haddock and Spinach Frittata

Prep time: 15 minutes
Cooking time: about 15 minutes

1 tbsp. vegetable oil

12oz. (350g) skinless smoked haddock, cut into chunks

4 handfuls baby spinach

8 extra-large eggs

4 tbsp. heavy cream

¼ tsp. freshly grated nutmeg

freshly ground black pepper

finely chopped fresh chives or parsley

½ cup grated cheddar cheese

mixed green salad to serve

1 Heat the oil in a 9in. (23cm) skillet with a flameproof handle and fry the fish, stirring occasionally, for 2 minutes. Add the spinach and cook for 3 minutes longer, or until wilted, trying not to break up the fish too much.

2 Heat the broiler to medium. Put the eggs, cream, nutmeg, and plenty of ground black pepper into a large bowl and beat together. Add most of the chives or parsley, if you like. Pour the egg mixture into the pan and use a wooden spoon to spread it evenly between the fish. Cook over low heat for 3–5 minutes until the egg is set around the edge.

3 Sprinkle the grated cheese over the frittata and broil for 3–5 minutes longer until the egg is cooked through and the cheese is golden and bubbling. Sprinkle with the remaining herbs, if you like. Cut the frittata into wedges and serve hot or at room temperature, with a mixed green salad.

Serves 4

Week 4 Shopping List

Chilled & Frozen

- [ ] 14oz. (400g) boneless beef suitable for stir-frying cut into strips
- [ ] 4 boneless, skinless chicken breast halves
- [ ] 12oz. (350g) skinless smoked haddock
- [ ] 11 eggs
- [ ] 2oz. (50g) Cheddar cheese
- [ ] 5oz. (150g) Jarlsberg cheese
- [ ] 13oz. (375g) piecrust dough, frozen or fresh
- [ ] 14oz. (400ml) heavy cream
- [ ] Orange juice, no pulp

Fruit, Vegetables, & Herbs

- [ ] 1 onion
- [ ] 2 large onions
- [ ] 1 head of garlic
- [ ] 2in. (5cm) piece of fresh ginger
- [ ] 3½oz. (100g) baby spinach
- [ ] 1 Savoy cabbage
- [ ] 11oz. (300g) mixed stir-fry vegetables
- [ ] 1 lemon
- [ ] Fresh chives (optional)
- [ ] Fresh parsley
- [ ] Mixed green salad leaves, to serve

Pantry
(In case you need to restock)
- ❑ Vegetable oil
- ❑ Olive oil
- ❑ Extra virgin olive oil
- ❑ All-purpose flour
- ❑ 1 can (2-oz./50g) anchovies in olive oil
- ❑ Soy sauce
- ❑ Wholegrain mustard
- ❑ 14oz. (400g) dried linguine or spaghetti
- ❑ Cornstarch
- ❑ Nutmeg
- ❑ Sesame seeds
- ❑ Sugar
- ❑ A few slices of white bread (for making bread crumbs)
- ❑ Applejack or apple cider
- ❑ Crusty bread, to serve
- ❑ Egg noodles, to serve
- ❑ Rice, to serve (optional)

Impress your Guests for Less

Planning Ahead

Planning will make your life easier when you're shopping on a budget. Unlike our grandmothers, who shopped daily and had little storage space, we have the refrigerator and freezer alongside our pantry.

Savvy shopping

Clever use of the refrigerator, freezer, and pantry makes life easier and shopping trips fewer. Nowadays, Sunday's roast doesn't have to be Monday's leftovers if it's prepared and put in the freezer for another day.

Change your shopping habits

❑ Do a big supermarket shop once a month for nonperishables—even better, order your shopping online to avoid impulse buys and keep an eye on the running total before you place the order. Some delivery companies offer free delivery at less popular times

❑ Top up with daily or weekly shops at supermarkets, independent stores, or farmer's markets for fresh ingredients

❑ Only buy special deals like "buy one, get one free" when you have time to batch cook or space to freeze the extra

❑ Avoid ready-made meals and prepared ingredients, such as chopped onions—you pay more for convenience

Before you go shopping

❑ Can you delay your food shopping for another day? Check the pantry, refrigerator, and freezer for ingredients to make another meal

❑ Check the diary and plan the week's menu according to family activities

❑ Do a quick weekly inventory of the pantry, refrigerator, and freezer. Can ingredients near their use-by or best-before date be incorporated into the week's menu?

❑ Don't forget nature's free bounty—gather blackberries, plums and sweet chestnuts, growing along the road, for example

The weekly menu

This needn't be a hefty document, simply jot down:

- ❑ An idea for every day of the week, including some dishes you've already made and stored in the refrigerator or freezer
- ❑ Some recipes that make creative use of leftovers
- ❑ Some recipes that stretch—pasta sauce tonight, chili tomorrow
- ❑ Some quick meals that need a trip to the shops for only one or two fresh ingredients
- ❑ Include vegetables or other accompaniments in your plan, but remember that you can always change your mind when you find a bargain in the supermarket
- ❑ Rethink your overall approach to cooking—meat and fish are expensive, so make one or two nights a week vegetarian, if you like

When you're shopping

- ❑ Tuck a notebook in your handbag listing ingredients for family favorites and you'll be ready to take advantage of special offers on expensive ingredients, such as meat and poultry
- ❑ Make a shopping list and stick to it
- ❑ Keep it seasonal (see pages 8–11)
- ❑ Think about if the product cost less whole or in portions—for example, it's cheaper to:
  - buy a whole chicken and cut it into pieces yourself (or ask your butcher to do it). Use the carcass for stock
  - cut a whole salmon into fillets or steaks, then freeze in portions
- ❑ Compare the price per pound. Loose fruit and vegetables can cost considerably less than the packaged versions, for example

Macaroni and Cheese

Prep time: 15 minutes
Cooking time: about 20 minutes

1lb. (450g) macaroni pasta

3 tbsp. butter

⅓ cup all-purpose flour

2 cups (500ml) 2 percent milk

1 cup grated sharp cheddar cheese

salt and freshly ground black pepper

½ cup fresh white bread crumbs

green salad to serve

1 Bring a large pot of salted water to a boil and cook the pasta for 5–8 minutes until just tender. Drain.

2 Meanwhile, melt the butter in a large saucepan. Stir in the flour and cook for 1 minute. Remove from the heat and gradually beat in the milk using a wooden spoon. Heat gently, stirring constantly, until the mixture thickens—3–5 minutes. Remove from the heat, stir in three-quarters of the cheese and the drained pasta. Season to taste with salt and pepper.

3 Heat the broiler to medium. Transfer the macaroni mixture to a 2-quart (2-liter) baking dish suitable for serving from and top with the remaining cheese and the bread crumbs. Broil for about 5 minutes until piping hot and golden. Serve immediately with a green salad.

Mushroom Linguine

Prep time: 10 minutes
Cooking time: about 10 minutes

14oz. (400g) dried linguine

1 tbsp. butter

5 cups slices cremini mushrooms

2 tbsp. pine nuts

1 tbsp. brandy (optional)

7 tbsp. mascarpone cheese

3 tbsp. freshly grated Parmesan cheese,
  plus extra to garnish

finely grated zest of 1 lemon

a large handful of baby spinach

salt and freshly ground black pepper

1 Cook the linguine according to the package directions. Drain, setting aside ⅔ cup (150ml) of the cooking water.

2 Meanwhile, heat the butter in a large skillet over high heat. Add the mushrooms and cook for 3–5 minutes. Add the pine nuts and cook for 1 minute. Stir in the brandy, if you like, and boil for 1 minute.

3 Add the mascarpone, Parmesan, reserved cooking water, and lemon zest to the pan, then stir in the spinach and linguine and cook until heated through. Season with salt and pepper, garnish with extra grated Parmesan and serve.

Serves 4

... and Chips with Minted Peas

Prep time: 15 minutes
Cooking time: about 40 minutes

4 large baking potatoes, about
   2lb. (900g) total

3 tbsp. vegetable oil

salt and freshly ground black pepper

3 tbsp. all-purpose flour

1 extra-large egg, beaten

2 cups fresh white bread crumbs

4 × 4oz. (125g) cod fillets, skinned

3 cups fresh or frozen shelled peas

1½ tbsp. thinly sliced fresh mint

tartar sauce, lemon wedges, and vinegar
   to serve

1 Preheat the oven to 400°F (350°F for convection ovens). Cut the potatoes into wedges and put on a large baking sheet. Drizzle with 1½ tbsp. of the oil, season well with salt and pepper, and toss to coat the wedges. Roast for 30–40 minutes until tender and golden brown.

2 Put the flour, egg, and bread crumbs in three separate shallow bowls.

3 When the wedges are 10 minutes away from being finished, bring a medium pot of water to a boil. Meanwhile, coat each fish fillet in flour, tapping off the excess, then dip into the egg and then into the bread crumbs.

4 Heat the remaining 1½ tbsp. oil in a large, nonstick skillet and cook the fish for 5 minutes, turning once, or until golden brown and cooked through.

5 Add the peas to the boiling water and cook for 2–3 minutes until tender. Drain. Using a potato masher, roughly crush the peas, then stir in the mint and season to taste with salt and pepper. Serve the fish immediately with a dollop of tartar sauce and a lemon wedge, plus the potato wedges and peas, and vinegar to sprinkle over.

Frozen fish fillets keep costs down. It's best to thaw them fully before using – in the refrigerator on a baking sheet lined with lots of paper towels is ideal.

Serves 4

Keep It Low Cost

It can be hard making sure that every member of the family eats healthy and balanced meals, especially if they come home at different times after various activities. Planning each week's menu in advance not only takes the stress out of deciding what to cook each day, but can save money in the long run.

Avoiding waste

By checking the pantry, planning your weekly menu, and always shopping with a list, you are well on your way to avoiding waste in the kitchen, as well as saving money. Yet, it's inevitable that there will be some leftovers from time to time; for example, if last-minute plans prevent you from eating a dinner that has already been planned for the week. A regular check of use-by dates of ingredients in the refrigerator should prevent this and planning ahead will help you to use them up in quick dinners or dishes to freeze for another day.

Expiration dates

These are a major area of debate. Supermarkets are extremely strict on expiration dates and will throw out any food the moment it is "out of date." Once you have purchased a product, you are asked to use it within the "use by" date. After this, you are encouraged to throw it out and start again. However, with the odd exception—and using your judgement on certain danger foods like fish and chicken—you can simply check if it's okay to use by smell, look, and feel. Follow your instincts: if it smells bad, toss it.

Portion sizes (per person)

As a rough guide, vegetables should half-fill the plate, while meat, fish, or poultry should take up one-quarter, with the remainder filled with carbohydrates, such as rice, pasta, or potatoes.

Soup	1¼ cups (300ml)

Fish, poultry, and meat
off the bone   6oz. (175g)

Whole chicken,   3lb. (1.4kg)
leg of lamb, or pork
should serve four with leftovers

Casseroles, stews
trimmed meat   8oz. (225g)

Shellfish
as main course   4oz. (125g)

Vegetables

- assuming you are serving three vegetables about ⅓ cup (2oz. /50g)
- assuming you are serving two vegetables a heaped ½ cup (3oz./75g)

Potatoes

small roast	3
mashed	heaped ¾ cup (6oz./175g)
new	¾ cup (4oz./125g)

Rice (as an accompaniment)
precooked quantity   ¼ cup

Couscous and bulgur wheat
(as an accompaniment)
precooked quantity   ¼ cup

Dried pasta   3–3½oz. (75–100g)

Salads   1 dessert bowl

k Carbonara

Prep time: 10 minutes
Cooking time: about 15 minutes

12oz. (350g) dried linguine

½ tbsp. olive oil

7oz. (200g) unsmoked back bacon, cut into ¼in. (0.5cm) pieces

4 extra-large eggs

6 tbsp. freshly grated Parmesan cheese, plus extra to serve

freshly ground black pepper

chopped fresh parsley to garnish

SAVE MONEY

This timeless recipe is usually made with cream, but this authentic version uses pasta cooking water for a meal that's lighter on your purse.

1 Bring a large pot of salted water to a boil and cook the linguine according to the package directions.

2 Meanwhile, heat the oil in a large skillet and fry the bacon for 5 minutes, or until golden. Remove from the heat.

3 Beat the eggs in a medium bowl with the Parmesan and plenty of ground black pepper. Drain the pasta, setting aside 7 tbsp. of the cooking water. Return the bacon pan back to low heat and stir in the pasta water, pasta, and egg mixture. Stir for 1 minute, or until thickened. Season with salt and pepper, garnish with a small handful of parsley and extra Parmesan, and serve.

Serves 4

Beef Quesadillas

Prep time: 15 minutes
Cooking time: about 45 minutes

½ tbsp. vegetable oil

5 scallions, thinly sliced

14oz. (400g) lean ground beef

a few dashes of Tabasco

¼ tsp. paprika

1 garlic clove, thinly sliced

2 cans (15oz./425g) crushed tomatoes

8 flour tortillas

1 cup grated sharp cheddar cheese

a large handful of fresh cilantro, roughly chopped

salt and freshly ground black pepper

lime wedges and sour cream to serve

1 Heat the oil in a large skillet. Fry the scallions for 3–5 minutes until just softened. Transfer to a large bowl. Brown the beef in the same pan over high heat for 5 minutes, or until cooked through. Stir in the Tabasco, paprika, and garlic and cook for 1 minute. Add the tomatoes and season to taste with salt and pepper, then simmer for 10 minutes. Add the beef mixture to the bowl with the scallions.

2 Wipe the pan clean, then put back over medium heat. Put a tortilla in the pan, then spoon on one-quarter each of the beef mixture, cheese, and cilantro. Top with another tortilla and heat through for 3 minutes.

3 Using a spatula or pancake turner, flip the quesadilla and cook on the other side for 3 minutes. Slide onto a cutting board, then cover with foil. Repeat with the remaining tortillas. Serve quartered, with lime wedges and sour cream.

Serves 4

Swedish Meatballs

Prep time: 15 minutes
Cooking time: about 15 minutes

1lb. 2oz. (500g) ground pork

1 tbsp. wholegrain mustard

1 extra-large egg

1½ cups fresh white bread crumbs

3 tbsp. finely chopped fresh dill

1 tbsp. vegetable oil

1¼ cups (300ml) chicken stock

⅔ cup (150ml) heavy cream

salt and freshly ground black pepper

cranberry sauce and boiled basmati rice
   to serve

1 Put the pork, mustard, egg, bread crumbs, and 2 tbsp. of the dill into a large bowl, season to taste with salt and pepper and mix well. Form into 20 golf ball-size balls.

2 Heat the oil in a large, deep skillet over medium heat. Fry the meatballs for 8–10 minutes until cooked through and golden.

3 Pour in the stock and cream, bring to a boil, and cook for 3 minutes. Sprinkle in the remaining dill and check the seasoning. Serve with cranberry sauce and rice.

Serves 4

Pork Schnitzel

Prep time: 15 minutes
Cooking time: about 5 minutes

4 thinly-cut, boneless pork loin chops

3 tbsp. all-purpose flour

2 eggs, beaten

3 cups fine fresh white bread crumbs

2 tbsp. sunflower oil

1 lemon, cut into wedges

green salad to serve

TRY THIS

For an easy variation on this Austrian favorite, just substitute chicken or turkey breasts, flattened.

1 Put one chop onto a cutting board and cover with plastic wrap. Using a rolling pin, gently hit the pork and flatten to an even thickness of ¼in. (0.5cm). Peel off the plastic wrap and let the pork dry on paper towels. Repeat with the remaining chops.

2 Put the flour, eggs, and bread crumbs in three separate shallow bowls. Coat each chop in flour, tapping off the excess, then dip into the beaten eggs followed by the bread crumbs.

3 Heat the oil in a large, nonstick skillet and fry the breaded chops for 5 minutes, turning once, or until golden and cooked through. Serve with lemon wedges and a green salad.

Sweet-and-Sour Pork Stir-Fry

Prep time: 15 minutes
Cooking time: about 10 minutes

2 tbsp. vegetable oil

12oz. (350g) pork tenderloin, cut into thin strips

1 red onion, thinly sliced

1 red bell pepper, seeded and thinly sliced

2 carrots, cut into thin strips

3 tbsp. sweet chili sauce

1 tbsp. white wine vinegar

½ cup chopped canned pineapple slices, with 2 tbsp. juice reserved

a large handful of bean sprouts

½ tbsp. sesame seeds

a large handful of fresh cilantro, roughly chopped

salt and freshly ground black pepper

boiled long-grain rice to serve

1 Heat the oil over high heat in a large skillet or wok. Add the pork, onion, red pepper, and carrots and cook for 3–5 minutes, stirring frequently, until the meat is cooked through and the vegetables are softening.

2 Stir in the chili sauce, vinegar, and reserved pineapple juice and bring to a boil, then stir in the pineapple chunks and bean sprouts and cook until heated through.

3 Season to taste with salt and pepper. Scatter the sesame seeds and cilantro over the mixture and serve immediately with rice.

SAVE TIME

As with all stir-fries, have everything sliced and ready before you start cooking.

Serves 4

Quick Curry

Prep time: 10 minutes
Cooking time: about 10 minutes

1 tbsp. sunflower oil

1 onion, thinly sliced

½ cup skinned and diced or thinly sliced
   chorizo

1 garlic clove, crushed

1 red chili pepper, seeded and thinly
   sliced (see Safety Tip, page 34)

1 tsp. garam masala

⅔ cup (150ml) coconut milk

2 cans (15-oz./425g) chickpeas, drained
   and rinsed

a large handful of spinach

salt and freshly ground black pepper

boiled basmati rice to serve

1 Heat the oil in a large pan and gently fry the onion for 5 minutes, or until softened. Add the chorizo, garlic, and chili and cook for 2 minutes, or until the chorizo is golden. Stir in the garam masala and cook for 1 minute longer.

2 Add the coconut milk, chickpeas, and ¾ cup plus 2 tbsp. water and cook until heated through. Stir in the spinach and season to taste with salt and pepper. Serve immediately with boiled rice.

Serves 4

ʼicken Kiev

Prep time: 15 minutes
Cooking time: about 25 minutes

4 tbsp. butter, softened

½ garlic clove, crushed

2 tbsp. finely chopped fresh parsley

salt and freshly ground black pepper

4 chicken breast halves

⅓ cup all-purpose flour

3 eggs, beaten

3½ cups fine fresh white bread crumbs

green salad to serve

1 Heat the oven to 400°F (350°F for convection ovens). Mix the butter with the garlic and parsley, and season to taste with salt and pepper. Cut a slit 1½in. (4cm) long and ½in. (1cm) deep in the top of each chicken breast. Press one-quarter of the butter mixture into each slit and secure with a wooden pick.

2 Put the flour, eggs, and bread crumbs in three separate shallow bowls. Coat each chicken breast in flour, tapping off the excess, then dip into the eggs and then into the bread crumbs. Finish by dipping each breast into the egg again before coating with a final layer of bread crumbs.

3 Put the breaded chicken breasts on a baking sheet and bake for 20–25 minutes until cooked through. Remove the wooden picks and serve immediately with a green salad.

Serves 4

Chicken Tagine

Prep time: 15 minutes
Cooking time: about 25 minutes

1 tbsp. vegetable oil

8 chicken drumsticks

½ tsp. each ground cumin, cilantro, cinnamon, and paprika

½ finely chopped dried apricots

½ cup raisins

1 can (15-oz./425g) crushed tomatoes

½ cup couscous

salt and freshly ground black pepper

a large handful of fresh cilantro, chopped, to garnish

1 Heat the oil in a large stovetop-safe casserole and brown the drumsticks well all over. Stir in the spices and cook for 1 minute. Add the apricots, raisins, tomatoes, 1¾ cups (400ml) water, and salt and pepper to taste, then bring to a boil and simmer for 10 minutes.

2 Stir in the couscous and simmer for 5 minutes longer, or until the couscous is tender and the chicken is cooked through. Check the seasoning. Sprinkle with chopped cilantro and serve immediately.

Serves 4

k Chicken

1 tbsp. fresh thyme leaves

1in. (2.5cm) piece of fresh ginger, peeled and grated

1 tsp. ground allspice

1 tbsp. white wine vinegar

1 tsp. soy sauce

1 garlic clove, crushed

2 green chili peppers, seeded and thinly chopped (see Safety Tip, page 34)

3 tbsp. vegetable oil

8 chicken pieces, such as thighs and drumsticks

boiled basmati rice and green salad or seasonal vegetables to serve

1 Heat the broiler to medium and set the broiler rack about 6in. (15cm) from the heat. Use a blender or a mortar and pestle to combine the thyme, ginger, allspice, vinegar, soy sauce, garlic, chili peppers, and oil until smooth.

2 Put the chicken pieces on a foil-lined baking sheet, then pour the jerk marinade over them and rub into the chicken. Broil for 12–15 minutes until golden and cooked through. Serve with rice and a green salad or seasonal vegetables.

Serves 4

Paella

Prep time: 15 minutes
Cooking time: about 30 minutes

1 tbsp. vegetable oil

1 large onion, thinly sliced

4 boneless, skinless chicken thighs, roughly chopped

2 garlic cloves, finely chopped

a pinch of saffron

¼ tsp. smoked paprika

1 red bell pepper, seeded and finely diced

1½ cups paella rice

4½ cups (1.1 liters) chicken stock, hot

6oz. (175g) shelled mussels

a large handful of fresh curly parsley, roughly chopped

salt and freshly ground black pepper

1 Gently heat the oil in a large paella pan or skillet and cook the onion for 5 minutes. Add the chicken and cook for 3 minutes. Stir in the garlic, saffron and paprika and cook for 1 minute to release the flavors.

2 Stir in the red pepper and rice. Pour in the hot stock and let simmer gently for 20 minutes, stirring occasionally, or until the rice is cooked through.

3 Stir in the mussels and parsley and season to taste with salt and pepper. Serve immediately.

Serves 4

From the Pantry

A Well-Stocked Storecupboard

A well-stocked pantry can help you rustle up a quick meal at short notice. However, resist the urge to fill the cupboards with interesting bottles that you "might use one day."

Stocking your pantry

Dried

- ❏ Pasta and noodles
- ❏ Rice (long-grain, Arborio and other risotto rice, pudding rice, paella rice)
- ❏ Beans
- ❏ Pizza crusts
- ❏ Nuts (pine nuts, walnuts, almonds)
- ❏ Dried fruit
- ❏ Bouillon cubes
- ❏ Spices and herbs
- ❏ Salt and ground black pepper
- ❏ Flour (all-purpose, bread, wholewheat, and self-rising)
- ❏ Cornstarch
- ❏ Dried yeast
- ❏ Gelatine
- ❏ Baking powder, cream of tartar, baking soda
- ❏ Sugar
- ❏ Tea and coffee
- ❏ Cocoa powder

Bottles and jars

- ❏ Mayonnaise
- ❏ Tomato ketchup and paste
- ❏ Tabasco sauce
- ❏ Worcestershire sauce
- ❏ Sweet chili sauce
- ❏ Pasta sauces
- ❏ Thai fish sauce
- ❏ Curry paste
- ❏ Chutneys
- ❏ Pickles
- ❏ Olives
- ❏ Capers
- ❏ Mustards
- ❏ Oils
- ❏ Vinegars
- ❏ Jam
- ❏ Marmalade
- ❏ Honey

Cans

- ❑ Crushed and whole tomatoes
- ❑ Fish (salmon, tuna, anchovies)
- ❑ Beans, chickpeas, and lentils
- ❑ Coconut milk
- ❑ Fruit

Variations

- Use 1 cup sun-dried tomatoes instead of the new potatoes.
- Throw in a handful of halved pitted black olives as you pour the egg into the pan.

Pantry Recipes

Pantry Omelet

A drizzle of olive oil or knob of butter, 1 finely chopped large onion, 1½ cups sliced cooked new potatoes, scant 1 cup thawed frozen baby peas, 6 beaten eggs, 5oz. (150g) sliced soft goat cheese, and salt and freshly ground black pepper.

1 Heat the oil or butter in a 10in. (25cm) nonstick, ovenproof skillet. Add the onion and fry for 6–8 minutes until golden. Add the potatoes and peas and cook, stirring, for 2–3 minutes. Heat the broiler.

2 Spread the vegetable mixture over the bottom of the skillet and pour in the eggs. Tilt the pan to coat the bottom with egg. Cook the omelet, undisturbed, for 2–3 minutes, then top with the cheese.

3 Put the pan under the hot broiler for 1–2 minutes until the egg is just set (no longer, or it will turn rubbery) and the cheese starts to turn golden. Season with salt and black pepper and serve.

Salmon and Pea Fish Cakes

Hands-on time: 15 minutes
Cooking time: about 10 minutes

⅔ cup frozen peas

15 soda crackers, about 4oz. (125g)

1 can (12¼-oz./360g) boneless, skinless salmon, drained

1 egg, separated

a few drops of Tabasco, to taste

1 tbsp. chopped fresh dill

1 tbsp. vegetable oil

3 tbsp. mayonnaise

2 tbsp. sweet chili sauce

salt and freshly ground black pepper

mixed green salad to serve

1 Put the peas into a bowl, cover with boiling water and let sit for a few minutes. Meanwhile, put five of the crackers into a food processor and pulse until finely ground. Transfer to a shallow plate and put to one side for the coating. Next, pulse the remaining whole crackers until finely ground. Add the salmon, egg yolk, Tabasco, dill, and plenty of salt and pepper to the processor and pulse again until combined. Drain the peas and add to the salmon mixture, then pulse briefly to combine.

2 Put the egg white into a shallow bowl and whisk lightly with a fork to break it up. Shape the fish mixture into four patties. Dip each one into the egg white, then coat in the reserved cracker crumbs.

3 Heat the oil in a large skillet and cook the fish cakes for 5 minutes on each side, or until piping hot and golden.

4 Meanwhile, stir the mayonnaise and chili sauce together in a small bowl. Serve the fish cakes with the dipping sauce and a mixed green salad.

TRY THIS

Soda crackers are an excellent substitute for bread crumbs and help to bind these easy fish cakes.

Serves 4

ne Puttanesca

12oz. (350g) dried penne pasta

1 tbsp. olive oil

1 onion, finely chopped

1 can (15-oz./425g) crushed tomatoes

2 tsp. dried oregano

4oz. (125g) canned boneless, skinless
    sardine fillets, drained

⅓ cup black olives, pitted

salt and freshly ground black pepper

a small handful of fresh curly parsley,
    chopped, to garnish

TRY THIS

Sardines give this dish substance
and texture, but in their place,
and to get a different dish, try
anchovies, the classic addition,
for their salty oomph.

1 Bring a large pot of salted water to a boil and cook the pasta according to the package directions. Drain well, setting aside a cupful of the cooking water.

2 Meanwhile, heat the oil in a large pan and fry the onion for 10 minutes, or until softened but not browned. Add the tomatoes and oregano, then bring the mixture to a boil, reduce the heat, and simmer for 15 minutes, or until thickened. Stir in the sardines and olives—the stirring should help break up the fish slightly.

3 Add the pasta to the sauce and toss well to combine. Add a little of the reserved pasta water if the mixture looks too dry. Season to taste with salt and pepper, then divide among four bowls and garnish with parsley. Serve immediately.

Serves 4

Cheesy Chicken and Vegetable Cobbler

Hands-on time: 20 minutes
Cooking time: about 20 minutes

7oz. (200g) cooked skinless chicken breast, cut into bite-size pieces

1⅓ cups frozen mixed vegetables

1¼ cups cream of tomato soup

1½ cups less 2 tbsp. self-rising flour, plus extra for dusting

½ tbsp. baking powder

½ cup grated sharp cheddar cheese

5 tbsp. milk, plus extra for brushing

1 egg, lightly beaten

½ tbsp. vegetable oil

salt and freshly ground black pepper

1 Heat the oven to 400°F (350°F for convection ovens). Put the cooked chicken, frozen vegetables, soup, and salt and pepper to taste into a medium bowl and stir to combine. Pour the mixture into a shallow 4¼-cup (1 liter) baking dish suitable for serving from and set aside.

2 Sift the flour, baking powder, and a large pinch of salt into a large bowl. Stir in most of the cheese. Beat the milk, egg, and oil together in a separate bowl.

3 Pour the milk mixture into the flour bowl and use a pastry blender to mix it together until the dough forms clumps. Add a splash of milk if it looks too dry.

4 Transfer the dough to a lightly floured work surface and pat it into a (roughly) 3½ × 6in. (9 × 15cm) rectangle. Cut the rectangle into eight equal squares, then arrange the biscuits on top of the chicken mixture. Brush each biscuit with a little milk, then sprinkle the remaining cheese on top.

5 Bake for 20 minutes, or until the biscuits are risen and golden and the filling is bubbling and piping hot. Serve immediately.

132

Serves 4

Make Your Own Stock

Good stock can make the difference between an ordinary dish and a great one. It gives depth of flavor to many dishes. There are four main types of stock: vegetable, meat, chicken and fish.

Vegetable Stock

For 4½ cups (1.1 liters), you will need:
1½ each chopped onion, celery, leek, and carrot, 2 bay leaves, a few fresh thyme sprigs, 1 small bunch of fresh parsley, 10 black peppercorns, and ½ tsp. salt.

1   Put all the ingredients into a pot and pour in 1¾ quarts (1.7 liters) cold water.
2   Bring slowly to a boil and skim the surface. Reduce the heat, partially cover the pot, and simmer gently for 30 minutes. Adjust the seasoning if necessary.
3   Strain the stock through a fine sieve into a bowl and let cool.

Chicken Stock

For 4½ cups (1.1 liters), you will need:
3½lb. (1.6kg) chicken bones or a stripped roast chicken carcass, 1½ cups each sliced onions and celery, ⅓ cup chopped leeks, 1 bouquet garni (2 bay leaves, a few fresh thyme sprigs, and a small bunch of fresh parsley), 1 tsp. black peppercorns, and ½ tsp. salt.

1   Put all the ingredients into a large pot with 3 quarts (3 liters) cold water.
2   Bring slowly to a boil and skim the surface. Reduce the heat, partially cover the pot, and simmer gently for 2 hours. Adjust the seasoning if necessary.
3   Strain the stock through a cheesecloth-lined sieve into a bowl and cool quickly. Defat (see opposite) before using.

Fish Stock

For 3¾ cups (900ml), you will need:
2lb. (900g) washed fish bones and
trimmings, 2 chopped carrots,
1 chopped onion, and 2 sliced celery
ribs, 1 bouquet garni (2 bay leaves,
a few fresh thyme sprigs, and a small
bunch of fresh parsley), 6 white
peppercorns, and ½ tsp. salt.

1 Put all the ingredients into a
   large pot with 3¾ cups (900ml)
   cold water.
2 Bring slowly to a boil and skim
   the surface. Reduce the heat,
   partially cover the pot and simmer
   gently for 30 minutes. Adjust the
   seasoning if necessary.
3 Carefully strain the stock through
   a cheesecloth-lined sieve into
   a bowl and cool quickly. Fish stock
   tends not to have much fat
   in it and so does not usually need
   to be defatted. However, if it does
   seem to be fatty, you will need
   to remove this by defatting
   it (see right).

Defatting stock

Meat and poultry stock needs to
be defatted. (Vegetable stock does
not.) You can mop the fat from the
surface using paper towels, but the
following methods are easier and
more effective. There are three main
methods that you can use: ladling,
pouring, and chilling.

1 **Ladling** While the stock is warm,
   place a ladle on the surface. Press
   down to allow the fat floating
   on the surface to trickle over the
   edge until the ladle is full. Discard
   the fat, then repeat until all the fat
   has been removed.
2 **Pouring** For this you need a fat
   separator, which has the spout
   at the bottom of the vessel. When
   you fill the fat separator with a fatty
   liquid, the fat rises. When you pour,
   the stock comes out while the fat
   stays behind in the jug.
3 **Chilling** This technique works
   best with stock made from meat,
   whose fat solidifies when cold. Put
   the cool stock in the refrigerator
   until the fat becomes solid, then
   remove the pieces of fat using
   a slotted spoon.

Steak and Guinness Pie

Hands-on time: 20 minutes
Cooking time: about 1 hour 25 minutes

14oz (400g) stewing beef, cut into
¾in (2cm) cubes

1oz (25g) all-purpose flour, plus extra
for dusting

1 tbsp vegetable oil

2 medium carrots, roughly chopped

1 onion, finely sliced

9fl oz (250ml) Guinness

9fl oz (250ml) beef stock

salt and freshly ground black pepper

2fl oz (50ml) heavy cream

1 tbsp red currant jelly

a small handful of fresh flat leaf parsley,
finely chopped

11oz (300g) bought puff pastry dough,
fresh or thawed

1 Put the beef into a bowl and coat with the flour. Heat the oil in a 6 pint (3.4 liter) Dutch oven or flameproof casserole and brown the beef, in batches if necessary, to keep the meat from steaming. Add the carrots and onion and cook for 3 minutes. Stir in the Guinness and stock and season to taste. Bring to a boil, then reduce the heat, cover and simmer for 30–40 minutes until the beef is tender, uncovering for the last 10 minutes.

2 Preheat the oven to 425°F (400°F for convection ovens). Stir the cream, red currant jelly, and parsley into the beef mixture and check the seasoning. Set aside.

3 Dust a work surface with flour and roll out the pastry to a thickness of ½in (1.5cm). Use the pastry to cover the pot, laying it on top of the beef mixture, then make a small slit in the middle of the pastry to let the steam escape. Bake for 25–30 minutes until the pastry is a golden brown. Serve immediately.

Serves 4

orn™ Lasagne

3 tbsp. olive oil

1 onion, finely chopped

1¼lb. (600g) frozen ground Quorn

7 tbsp. dry red wine

2 cans (15-oz./425g) crushed tomatoes

1½ tbsp. Italian seasoning

1 vegetable bouillon cube

4 tbsp. all-purpose flour

salt and freshly ground black pepper

2½ cups (600ml) milk

9 no-boil lasagne noodles

½ cup grated sharp cheddar cheese,

green salad to serve

1 Heat 1 tbsp. of the oil in a large pan and fry the onion for 10 minutes. or until softened. Turn up the heat, add the Quorn and fry for 5 minutes, or until golden. Add the wine and simmer for 5 minutes.

2 Stir in the tomatoes and Italian seasoning, then crumble in the bouillon cube and season with salt and pepper to taste. Bring the mixture to a boil, then reduce the heat and simmer for 5 minutes, or until thickened. Remove from the heat.

3 Next, make the white sauce. Heat the remaining oil in a small pan and stir in the flour. Cook for 30 seconds, then remove the pan from the heat and gradually whisk in the milk. Return the milk mixture to the stovetop and bring to a boil, then reduce the heat and simmer for 5 minutes, whisking, or until thickened and glossy.

4 Heat the oven to 400°F (350°F for convection ovens). Spoon one-third of the Quorn mixture into the bottom of a 2-quart (2 liter) baking dish suitable for serving from. Cover with three lasagne noodles and a little white sauce. Repeat the layering process twice more, finishing with a layer of white sauce. Sprinkle the cheese over and bake for 30–35 minutes until bubbling and golden (cover with tin foil if browning too quickly). Serve with a green salad.

Serves 6

Sticky Ribs with Rice and Beans

Hands-on time: 15 minutes
Cooking time: about 55 minutes

scant 1 cup ketchup

1½ tbsp. soy sauce

1½ tbsp. white wine vinegar

3 tbsp. honey

1½ tsp. pumpkin pie spice

½ tsp. cayenne pepper, or to taste

3lb. 2oz. (1.5kg) individual pork spareribs

1¼ cups basmati rice

1 can (15-oz./425g) kidney beans, drained and rinsed

a large handful of fresh cilantro, chopped

green salad to serve

TRY THIS

Use this delicious glaze on grilled or broiled sausages or sizzling pork for a twist on this recipe.

1 Heat the oven to 400°F (350°F for convection ovens). Line a large roasting pan with a double layer of tin foil. Put the first six ingredients into a large bowl and stir to combine. Add the ribs to the bowl and stir to coat completely, then empty the ribs and glaze into the prepared roasting pan and spread out evenly. Cover with foil and roast for 20 minutes.

2 Uncover the pan and turn the ribs over, then put back into the oven for 30–35 minutes, turning in the glaze occasionally, until they're dark and sticky. (Most of the liquid should have evaporated.)

3 Meanwhile, cook the rice according to the package directions, adding the kidney beans for the final 2 minutes of cooking. Drain well and stir in the cilantro. Serve the rice with the ribs and a green salad.

Serves 4

Make It Go Farther

Before going shopping, have a good look at the ingredients in your refrigerator and vegetable drawer and think of ways to use them. You can then buy the ingredients you need to make the most of what you already have.

Clever leftovers

We all struggle with portion size and often have extra rice, potatoes, or other ingredients left at the end of each meal. There is a difference between leftovers and wasted food. Leftovers are the bits and pieces that sit in a plastic-wrap-covered bowl in your refrigerator, challenging you to use them creatively. If you ignore them for four or five days they become waste. Why not try making the most of your leftover tidbits?

Ways of using leftovers

There are many ways of using leftover food and slightly overripe fruit and vegetables that are starting to wilt. You can:

- ❑ Simply add the ingredients to a stir-fry, pasta, soup, risotto...the list is endless
- ❑ "Stretch" the ingredients— sometimes the amount left over is so small it won't go very far in a family setting. You can cook a little more of the same ingredient (rice, for example), or try adding lentils and tomatoes to leftover ground beef to create a whole new take on a classic pasta sauce
- ❑ Make the most of fruit and vegetables that are past their prime—use fruit in a crumble; use vegetables in soups and casseroles

Alternative suggestions

You might not always feel like transforming your leftovers into meals—or there may not be enough to do so. Another option is to freeze the odd ingredient for later use.

Small amounts of herbs—freeze in ice cube trays

One or two chilies—these freeze well and are easy to chop when frozen

Heavy cream—lightly whip the cream and then freeze

Cheese—hard cheeses will become crumbly once thawed, but can be used for grating or in cooking

Bread—blend in a food processor to make bread crumbs: these freeze well in a sealed plastic bag. Use to sprinkle over casseroles for a crisp topping, or to coat fish or chicken before frying, broiling, or baking—or use for bread stuffing to serve with game or turkey

Leftover Roast Chicken Soup

3 tbsp. olive oil, 1 chopped onion, 1 chopped carrot, 2 chopped celery ribs, 2 chopped fresh thyme sprigs, 1 bay leaf, a stripped roast chicken carcass, 1–1½ cups chopped roast chicken, 1 cup mashed or roast potatoes, 1 tbsp. heavy cream, salt and freshly ground black pepper.

1   Heat the oil in a large pot. Add the onion, carrot, celery, and thyme and fry gently for 20–30 minutes until soft, but not brown. Add the bay leaf, chicken carcass and 3¾ cups (900ml) boiling water to the pan. Bring to a boil, then reduce the heat and simmer for 5 minutes.
2   Remove the bay leaf and carcass and add the chopped roast chicken and cooked potato to the pot. Simmer for 5 minutes.
3   Blend the soup in a food processor, pour back into the pot and bring to a boil. Stir in the cream, season to taste with salt and pepper, and serve immediately.

Cheap Desserts

Apple Galette

Hands-on time: 20 minutes
Cooking time: about 35 minutes

all-purpose flour for dusting

1lb. 2oz. (500g) bought puff pastry dough, fresh or thawed

8 tbsp. apricot jam

4 cooking apples, such as Braeburn, cored and very thinly sliced

whipped cream or ice cream to serve (optional)

FREEZE AHEAD

Complete the recipe, then cool the finished, glazed tart and cut into slices. Wrap each slice well in nonstick paper and freeze for up to 1 month. (Wrapped slices can be stacked on top of each other.) To serve, thaw at room temperature (about 1 hour) or arrange the frozen slices on a baking sheet and reheat in a preheated 300°F (275°F for convection ovens) oven for 15–20 minutes until thawed.

1 Heat the oven to 400°F (350°F for convection ovens). Lightly dust a work surface with flour and roll out the dough until it measures roughly 10 × 14in. (25 × 35.5cm) and is ¼in. (0.5cm) thick. Trim the edges to straighten them if needed. Put onto a cookie sheet and prick the dough all over with a fork, leaving a ½in. (1cm) border unpricked around the edges.

2 Spread half the jam over the pricked dough, then arrange the apple slices on top, overlapping them to make neat rows.

3 Bake the tart for 30–35 minutes until the pastry is golden and the apples have just started to take on color. When the tart is 5 minutes away from the end of the baking time, heat the remaining jam with 2 tsp. water until just boiling, then carefully brush over the apples as soon as you take the tart out of the oven. Serve in slices, warm or at room temperature, with whipped cream or ice cream, if you like.

Cuts into 8 pieces

Rhubarb and Ginger Cheesecake

Hands-on time: 25 minutes, plus chilling
Cooking time: about 2 hours, plus cooling

3¾ cups rhubarb cut into chunks

4 tbsp. sugar

2 balls preserved stem ginger, syrup reserved

6oz (175g) ginger snaps, finely crushed

4 tbsp. unsalted butter, melted

2 cups cream cheese

3 eggs

1 tsp. vanilla extract

4 tbsp. confectioners' sugar

½ tsp. arrowroot starch

1 Put half of the rhubarb chunks into a pan with the sugar, 3 tbsp. reserved ginger syrup, and 2 tbsp. cold water. Simmer for 5–10 minutes until tender. Transfer to a food processor and blend until smooth, then let cool.

2 Finely chop the stem ginger and combine with the gingersnaps and butter. Press into the bottom of a 7in. (18cm) round springform pan, then chill until firm.

3 Heat the oven to 300°F (275°F for convection ovens). Whisk together the cream cheese, eggs, vanilla extract, and 3 tbsp. of the confectioners' sugar. Fold in two-thirds of the rhubarb puree. Pour into the cake pan. Stir the remaining puree through the filling, making swirls and ripples. Bake for 1½ hours, or until just set, then leave in the oven with the door ajar until cool. Chill, preferably overnight.

4 Put the remaining rhubarb into a pan with ⅔ cup (150ml) cold water, the remaining confectioners' sugar, and 2 tbsp. ginger syrup. Poach gently for 5–10 minutes until just tender. Remove the rhubarb and set aside, then strain the liquid into a bowl and pour it back into the rinsed-out pan. Mix 1 tbsp. of the liquid with the arrowroot starch until smooth, then add to the rest. Bring to a boil, then remove from the heat as soon as it is slightly thickened and let cool.

5 To serve, remove the cheesecake from the pan and top with the poached rhubarb. Slice and drizzle with the sauce.

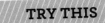

TRY THIS

Crush the biscuits to a fine powder in a food processor. Alternatively, put them into a plastic bag and crush with a rolling pin.

Cuts into 8 slices

Bread-and-Butter Pudding

Hands-on time: 10 minutes, plus soaking
Cooking time: about 40 minutes

4 tbsp. butter, softened, plus extra
for greasing

10oz. (275g) white country-style bread,
crusts removed, cut into
½in. (1cm) slices

⅓ cup raisins

3 eggs

scant 2 cups (450ml) milk

3 tbsp. confectioners' sugar, plus extra
for dusting

1 Lightly grease four 1¼-cup (300ml) gratin dishes or one 4½-cup (1.1 liter) baking dish suitable for serving from. Butter the bread, then cut into quarters to make triangles. Arrange the bread in the dish(es) and sprinkle with the raisins.

2 Beat the eggs, milk, and sugar in a bowl. Pour the mixture over the bread and let to soak for 10 minutes. Heat the oven to 350°F (300°F for convection ovens).

3 Bake the pudding(s) in the oven for 30–40 minutes. Dust with confectioners' sugar to serve.

Serves 4

...ezer Feast Banoffee Cheesecake

Hands-on time: 25 minutes, plus chilling
Cooking time: about 1 hour 5 minutes, plus cooling

For the crust

7 tbsp. butter, melted, plus extra
   for greasing
2⅓ cups finely crushed Graham crackers

For the filling

2 small very ripe bananas, about
   5oz. (150g) peeled weight
2¼ cups full-fat cream cheese
1 cup superfine sugar
1½ tbsp. all-purpose flour
1 tsp. vanilla extract
2 eggs, separated

To decorate

3 tbsp. caramel sauce
1oz. (25g) semisweet chocolate, shaved
   into flakes with a vegetable peeler

1 Heat the oven to 350°F (325°F for
convection ovens). Grease an 8in.
(20cm) round springform pan and
line the bottom with parchment paper.
Mix together the butter and crushed
crumbs, then press into the bottom
of the pan. Bake for 15 minutes, then
remove from the oven and set aside.
Reduce the oven temperature to 325°F
(300°F for convection ovens).

2 To make the filling, blend the bananas
in a food processor until smooth.
Add the rest of the filling ingredients
except the egg whites to the processor
and blend again until smooth.
Transfer the mixture to a large bowl.
In a separate, clean bowl, whisk the
egg whites until they hold soft peaks.
Using a large metal spoon, fold them
into the banana mixture.

3 Pour the mixture into the pan and
shake gently to level. Bake for
50 minutes, or until the cheesecake
is lightly golden—the filling will
be wobbly, but will firm up when
chilled. Working quickly, take the
cheesecake out of the oven and run
a small knife around the side of the
cheesecake to release it. (This should
help minimize cracking.) Let cool for
30 minutes (don't worry if a few cracks

appear, they will be covered with the topping) and chill for at least 2 hours, or overnight.

4 Remove the cheesecake from the pan, peel off the parchment paper and transfer to a serving plate. Allow the cheesecake to come to room temperature—about 1 hour.

5 Put the caramel into a small bowl and whisk briefly to loosen it, then drizzle it over the top of the cheesecake. Scatter the chocolate flakes over and serve in slices.

FREEZE AHEAD

Prepare the cheesecake to the end of step 3. Wrap the cooled cheesecake (still in its pan) well with plastic wrap and freeze for up to one month. To serve, let it thaw in the refrigerator, then unwrap and finish the recipe.

Serves 8

Perfect Eggs

Eggs are a wonderfully versatile ingredient that can make a perfect dessert.
All you need to remember with crepe batter is to mix quickly and lightly.
For a simple yet sublime meringue, you need just egg whites
and sugar. Easy!

Perfect Crepes

To make eight crepes, you will need:
1 cup all-purpose flour, a pinch of
salt, 1 egg, 1¼ cups (300ml) milk,
vegetable oil, and butter to fry.

1 Sift the flour and salt into a bowl,
   make a well in the middle and
   whisk in the egg. Gradually beat
   in the milk to make a smooth
   batter, then let stand for
   20 minutes.
2 Heat a heavy-bottomed skillet and
   coat lightly with oil and butter.
   Pour in a little batter and tilt the
   pan to coat the bottom thinly
   and evenly.
3 Cook over medium-high heat
   for 1 minute, or until golden. Flip
   carefully and cook the other side
   for 30 seconds to 1 minute.

Perfect Meringues

Baking meringues is best done whenever you know you won't be needing your oven for a good few hours, because after baking they must be left to dry in the turned-off oven for several hours or overnight.

To make 12 meringues, you will need: 3 egg whites and ¾ cup plus 2 tbsp. superfine sugar.

1 Heat the oven to 325°F (300°F for convection ovens). Line a cookie sheet with parchment paper.
2 Put the egg whites into a large, clean bowl and whisk until soft peaks form. Add a spoonful of sugar and whisk until glossy.
3 Keep adding the sugar a spoonful at a time, whisking thoroughly after each addition, until you have used half the sugar. The mixture should be thick and glossy.
4 Sprinkle the remaining sugar over the mixture and then, using a metal spoon, gently fold it in.
5 Hold a large spoon in each hand and pick up a spoonful of mixture in one spoon, then scrape the other spoon against it to lift the mixture off. Repeat the process a few times, to form a rough oval shape. Using the empty spoon, push the oval onto the prepared cookie sheet—hold it just over the sheet so that it doesn't drop from a great height. Continue this process with the remaining mixture to make 12 meringues.
6 Put the meringues into the oven and bake for 15 minutes, then turn the oven off and leave them in the oven to dry out for several hours or overnight.

3

Microwave Meringues

TAKE 5

Hands-on time: 15 minutes
Cooking time: 2 minutes

1 tbsp. egg white

1¼ cups confectioners' sugar

1 cup heavy cream

2 tbsp. gated white chocolate

⅓ cup raspberries

1 Put the egg white into a large bowl, then sift in the confectioners' sugar. Mix briefly with a wooden spoon (don't whisk), then use your hands to bring the mixture together—it will be very stiff. (Don't be tempted to add more egg white.) Knead until smooth.

2 Divide the mixture into 16 equal pieces and roll each piece into a ball. Line the turntable of the microwave with parchment paper, then arrange four balls on the parchment, spacing them evenly apart.

3 Microwave on full power for exactly 40 seconds. (If, however, your microwave is old, this can take longer). Slide the parchment and meringues out of the microwave and repeat the process with the remaining balls.

4 Whip the cream and chocolate together until the mixture just holds its shape. Briefly whip in the raspberries to create a marbling effect, then use the mixture to sandwich the meringues together. Serve.

Serves 8

Cheat's Chocolate Soufflés

Hands-on time: 15 minutes
Cooking time: about 12 minutes

butter for greasing

3oz. (75g) bittersweet chocolate

1 cup fresh chocolate pudding

3 egg whites

2 tbsp. superfine sugar

confectioners' sugar to dust

1 Heat the oven to 425°F (400°F for convection ovens). Put a baking sheet on the middle shelf to heat up, making sure there's enough space for the soufflés to rise. Grease six ½-cup (125ml) ramekins.

2 Finely grate the chocolate, or pulse in a food processor until it resembles bread crumbs. Dust the insides of the ramekins with one-third of the chocolate.

3 Mix the pudding and remaining chocolate together in a large bowl. In a separate, grease-free bowl, whisk the egg whites until stiff but not dry, then gradually add the superfine sugar to the egg whites, whisking well after each addition. Using a metal spoon, fold the egg whites into the pudding mixture.

4 Quickly divide the mixture among the prepared ramekins. Put them onto the heated baking sheet and bake for 10–12 minutes until well risen. Dust the soufflés with confectioners' sugar and serve immediately.

Serves 6

Luscious Lemon Passion Pots

⅔ cup (150g) sweetened condensed milk

4 tbsp. heavy whipping cream

grated zest and juice of 1 large lemon

1 passion fruit

1 Put the condensed milk, heavy cream, and lemon zest and juice into a medium bowl and whisk until thick and fluffy. Spoon into two small ramekins or coffee cups and chill until needed—or continue with the recipe if you can't wait.

2 To serve, halve the passion fruit, scoop out the seeds, and use to decorate the lemon pots.

Serves 2

Make Your Own Ice Cream

Rich and creamy, fresh and fruity, or sweet and indulgent, ice creams and iced desserts are easy to make. Good ice cream should have a smooth, creamy texture. Using an ice-cream maker is the best way to achieve it, but freezing and breaking up the ice crystals by hand works well, too.

Vanilla Ice Cream

To serve four to six, you will need: 1¼ cups (300ml) milk, 1 vanilla bean, split lengthwise, 3 egg yolks, 6 tbsp. superfine sugar, 1¼ cups (300ml) heavy cream.

1 Put the milk and vanilla bean into a pan and heat slowly until almost boiling. Remove from the heat and let sit for 20 minutes, then remove the vanilla bean. Whisk the egg yolks and sugar in a large bowl until thick and creamy. Gradually whisk in the milk, then strain back into the pan.

2 Cook over low heat, stirring with a wooden spoon, until thick enough to coat the back of the spoon—do not boil. Pour into a chilled bowl and let cool.

3. Whisk the cream into the custard. Pour into an ice-cream maker and freeze or churn according to the manufacturer's directions, or make by hand (see below, right). Store in an airtight container for up to one week. Put the ice cream in the refrigerator for 15–20 minutes before serving to soften slightly.

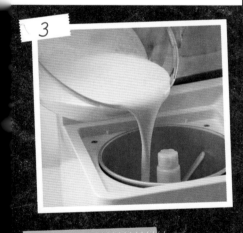

3

TRY THIS

Once you've made the custard, you can make different flavored ice cream.

Variations

Fruit Ice Cream: sweeten 1¼ cups (300ml) fruit puree—such as rhubarb, gooseberry, raspberry, or strawberry —to taste, then stir into the cooked custard and churn.

Chocolate Ice Cream: omit the vanilla and add 4oz. (125g) bittersweet chocolate to the milk. Heat gently until melted, then bring almost to a boil and proceed as for Vanilla Ice Cream.

Coffee Ice Cream: omit the vanilla bean and add ⅔ cup (150ml) cooled strong coffee to the cooked custard and churn.

Making ice cream by hand

1. Pour the ice-cream mixture into a shallow container, cover, and freeze until partially frozen.
2. Spoon into a bowl and mash with a fork to break up the ice crystals. Put back into the container and freeze for 2 hours longer. Repeat and freeze for another 3 hours.

Three-Ingredient Strawberry Ice Cream

Hands-on time: 10 minutes

1lb. 2oz. (500g) hulled and frozen strawberries

heaped ½ cup confectioners' sugar

½ cup (125ml) heavy cream

1. Put all the ingredients into a food processor. Pulse until the strawberries are fairly broken down, then blend until the mixture is smooth.
2. Serve immediately or transfer to an airtight container and freeze for up to one week. Allow to soften a little at room temperature before serving.

SAVE TIME

You can make this in advance and keep in an airtight container in the freezer for up to three days.

Serves 6

Cheat's Chocolate Fudge

TAKE
5

🍴 **Hands-on time:** 10 minutes
Cooking time: 2 minutes, plus chilling

---

heaped 4 cups confectioners' sugar

heaped ½ cup cocoa powder, sifted

4 tbsp. milk

4 tbsp. cold butter, chopped

a large handful of roasted and
salted peanuts

1 Put the confectioners' sugar and cocoa powder into a large, microwave-safe bowl and whisk to combine. Add the milk and butter and microwave on full power for 2 minutes.

2 Meanwhile, line an 8in. (20cm) square cake pan or baking dish with parchment paper.

3 Whisk the hot mixture until smooth, which will thicken as you do so, then stir in the nuts. Transfer to the prepared pan, smooth the surface, and chill for 20 minutes until solid. Serve in squares.

Cuts into 24 squares

Lemon Meringue Pie

Hands-on time: 30 minutes, plus chilling
Cooking time: about 1 hour, plus standing

For the pastry

1¾ cups plus 2 tbsp. all-purpose flour, plus extra for dusting

a pinch of salt

1¼ sticks butter, cut into pieces

1 egg yolk

2 tbsp. superfine sugar

a little beaten egg to brush

For the filling and topping

7 eggs, 4 separated, at room temperature

finely grated zest of 3 lemons

¾ cup (175ml) freshly squeezed lemon juice (about 4 lemons), strained

1¾ cups (400ml) sweetened condensed milk

⅔ cup (150ml) heavy cream

heaped 1¾ cups confectioners' sugar

TRY THIS

To make a lime meringue pie, use lime zest and juice instead of lemon.

1 Sift the flour and salt into a clean mound on a clean work surface. Make a large well in the middle and add the butter, egg yolk, sugar, and 3 tbsp. cold water. Using the fingertips of one hand, work the butter, egg yolk, sugar, and water together until well blended. Gradually work in all the flour to bind the mixture together. Knead the dough gently on a lightly floured surface until smooth, wrap in plastic wrap, and let rest in the refrigerator for at least 30 minutes before rolling out.

2 Roll out the dough on a lightly floured surface and use to line a 9in. (23cm), 1½in. (4cm) deep, fluted tart pan with a removable bottom. Prick the bottom with a fork and chill for 30 minutes. Meanwhile, heat the oven to 375°F (325°F for convection ovens).

3 Bake the pie shell blind for 10 minutes. Brush the inside with beaten egg and put back into the oven for 1 minute to seal. Increase the oven temperature to 350°F (325°F for convection ovens).

4 To make the filling, put 4 egg yolks into a bowl with the 3 whole eggs. Add the lemon zest and juice and whisk lightly. Stir in the condensed milk and cream.

5 Pour the filling into the pie shell and bake for 30 minutes, or until just set in the middle. Let cool while you prepare the meringue. Increase the oven temperature to 400°F (350°F for convection ovens).

6 For the meringue, using a hand-held electric mixer, whisk the egg whites and confectioners' sugar together in a heatproof bowl over a pan of simmering water for 10 minutes, or until shiny and thick. Remove from the heat and continue to whisk at low speed for 5–10 minutes until the bowl is cool. Pile the meringue onto the filling and swirl to form peaks. Bake for 5–10 minutes until the meringue is lightly browned. Let stand for about 1 hour, then serve.

Serves 8

453 cal ♥ 22g protein
25g fat (6g sat) ♥ 3g fiber
38g carb ♥ 1.6g salt

12

389 cal ♥ 17g protein
18g fat (10g sat) ♥ 2g fiber
41g carb ♥ 2.8g salt

14

432 cal ♥ 20g protein
20g fat (7g sat) ♥ 5g fiber
46g carb ♥ 1.8g salt

18

121 cal ♥ 5g protein
6g fat (1g sat) ♥ 2g fiber
11g carb ♥ 0.9g salt

20

223 cal ♥ 9g protein
10g fat (2g sat) ♥ 1g fiber
22g carb ♥ 1.4g salt

34

339 cal ♥ 26g protein
11g fat (2g sat) ♥ 3g fiber
37g carb ♥ 0.4g salt

36

240 cal ♥ 15g protein
9g fat (2g sat) ♥ 3g fiber
25g carb ♥ 1.6g salt

38

517 cal ♥ 34g protein
21g fat (8g sat) ♥ 6g fiber
51g carb ♥ 0.8g salt

52

654 cal ♥ 12g protein
35g fat (18g sat) ♥ 5g fiber
67g carb ♥ 3.3g salt

56

313 cal ♥ 22g protein
16g fat (4g sat) ♥ 7g fiber
24g carb ♥ 1.8g salt

58

513 cal ♥ 35g protein
19g fat (7g sat) ♥ 5g fiber
54g carb ♥ 1.1g salt

70

324 cal ♥ 26g protein
15g fat (4g sat) ♥ 2g fiber
24g carb ♥ 1.3g salt

72

349 cal ♥ 20g protein
16g fat (5g sat) ♥ 10g fiber
34g carb ♥ 3.3g salt

74

519 cal ♥ 33g protein
14g fat (4g sat) ♥ 3g fiber
65g carb ♥ 1.3g salt

76

506 cal ♥ 10g protein
33g fat (5g sat) ♥ 4g fiber
46g carb ♥ 1.2g salt

24

197 cal ♥ 4g protein
8g fat (1g sat) ♥ 3g fiber
29g carb ♥ 1.3g salt

26

76 cal ♥ 2g protein
3g fat (0.5g sat) ♥ 2g fiber
11g carb ♥ 0.1g salt

28

261 cal ♥ 23g protein
16g fat (10g sat) ♥ 1g fiber
9g carb ♥ 2.3g salt

32

474 cal ♥ 8g protein
15g fat (4g sat) ♥ 4g fiber
79g carb ♥ 1.3g salt

44

560 cal ♥ 35g protein
30g fat (5g sat) ♥ 3g fiber
40g carb ♥ 0.9g salt

46

485 cal ♥ 12g protein
33g fat (17g sat) ♥ 1g fiber
27g carb ♥ 1.5g salt

48

478 cal ♥ 30g protein
26g fat (9g sat) ♥ 0.6g fiber
19g carb ♥ 2.8g salt

50

398 cal ♥ 25g protein
19g fat (9g sat) ♥ 1g fiber
21g carb ♥ 1.1g salt

60

591 cal ♥ 39g protein
31g fat (17g sat) ♥ 4g fiber
41g carb ♥ 1.3g salt

62

461 cal ♥ 37g protein
28g fat (11g sat) ♥ 0.4g fiber
10g carb ♥ 1.2g salt

64

532 cal ♥ 25g protein
19g fat (9g sat) ♥ 4g fiber
71g carb ♥ 1.8g salt

68

220 cal ♥ 23g protein
10g fat (3g sat) ♥ 2g fiber
8g carb ♥ 0.7g salt

80

421 cal ♥ 40g protein
25g fat (14g sat) ♥ 0.9g fiber
6g carb ♥ 1.0g salt

82

475 cal ♥ 17g protein
9g fat (1g sat) ♥ 6g fiber
87g carb ♥ 1.6g salt

84

933 cal ♥ 23g protein
71g fat (32g sat) ♥ 3g fiber
56g carb ♥ 2.5g salt

86

390 cal ♥ 35g protein
28g fat (11g sat) ♥ 0.5g fiber
1g carb ♥ 2.4g salt

88

703 cal ♥ 27g protein
24g fat (14g sat) ♥ 4g fiber
102g carb ♥ 1.3g salt

96

582 cal ♥ 19g protein
23g fat (12g sat) ♥ 4g fiber
76g carb ♥ 0.9g salt

98

587 cal ♥ 40g protein
17g fat (3g sat) ♥ 9g fiber
76g carb ♥ 1.3g salt

100

282 cal ♥ 21g protein
15g fat (3g sat) ♥ 3g fiber
16g carb ♥ 1.9g salt

112

437 cal ♥ 18g protein
28g fat (15g sat) ♥ 7g fiber
31g carb ♥ 1.7g salt

114

480 cal ♥ 50g protein
17g fat (7g sat) ♥ 1g fiber
48g carb ♥ 1.8g salt

116

254 cal ♥ 27g protein
6g fat (1g sat) ♥ 2g fiber
27g carb ♥ 0.9g salt

118

372 cal ♥ 27g protein
12g fat (4g sat) ♥ 2g fiber
42g carb ♥ 2.2g salt

132

591 cal ♥ 26g protein
34g fat (16g sat) ♥ 1g fiber
42g carb ♥ 1.5g salt

136

539 cal ♥ 36g protein
19g fat (5g sat) ♥ 12g fiber
58g carb ♥ 2.5g salt

138

447 cal ♥ 18g protein
7g fat (3g sat) ♥ 4g fiber
82g carb ♥ 1.9g salt

140

247 cal ♥ 1g protein
18g fat (11g sat) ♥ 0.2g fiber
22g carb ♥ 0g salt

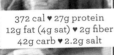

156

126 cal ♥ 3g protein
5g fat (2g sat) ♥ 0.4g fiber
19g carb ♥ 0.1g salt

158

377 cal ♥ 7g protein
21g fat (13g sat) ♥ 0.3g fiber
43g carb ♥ 0.3g salt

160

175 cal ♥ 1g protein
11g fat (7g sat) ♥ 0.9g fiber
18g carb ♥ 0g salt

164

598 cal ♥ 33g protein
25g fat (9g sat) ♥ 3g fiber
65g carb ♥ 2.2g salt

104

650 cal ♥ 40g protein
33g fat (15g sat) ♥ 4g fiber
55g carb ♥ 2.2g salt

106

544 cal ♥ 29g protein
39g fat (18g sat) ♥ 0.4g fiber
21g carb ♥ 1.1g salt

108

411 cal ♥ 26g protein
24g fat (7g sat) ♥ 0.7g fiber
24g carb ♥ 0.7g salt

110

327 cal ♥ 19g protein
26g fat (6g sat) ♥ 0g fiber
1g carb ♥ 0.1g salt

120

425 cal ♥ 21g protein
6g fat (1g sat) ♥ 2g fiber
67g carb ♥ 0.9g salt

122

373 cal ♥ 23g protein
22g fat (4g sat) ♥ 2g fiber
23g carb ♥ 2.0g salt

128

427 cal ♥ 18g protein
9g fat (2g sat) ♥ 4g fiber
72g carb ♥ 1.6g salt

130

344 cal ♥ 4g protein
16g fat (10g sat) ♥ 0.9g fiber
45g carb ♥ 0.5g salt

146

530 cal ♥ 6g protein
39g fat (23g sat) ♥ 1g fiber
40g carb ♥ 0.9g salt

148

691 cal ♥ 6g protein
50g fat (29g sat) ♥ 0.8g fiber
57g carb ♥ 0.9g salt

450 cal ♥ 16g protein
13g fat (5g sat) ♥ 1g fiber
70g carb ♥ 1.1g salt

150

152

111 cal ♥ 1g protein
3g fat (2g sat) ♥ 0.4g fiber
22g carb ♥ 0.1g salt

166

692 cal ♥ 14g protein
36g fat (21g sat) ♥ 0.9g fiber
83g carb ♥ 0.6g salt

168

Index

PICTURE CREDITS

Photographers: Steve Baxter (pages 15, 19, 25, 27, 33, 35, 97, 99, 101, 105, 107, 109, 111, 113, 115, 117, 119, 121, 123, 129, 131, 133, 137, 139 and 141); Martin Brigdale (page 37); Nicki Dowey (page 39); Gareth Morgans (pages 45, 47, 49, 51, 53, 57, 59, 61, 63, 65, 69, 71, 73, 75, 77, 81, 83, 85, 87, 89, 147, 153, 159, 161 and 165); Myles New (pages 157 and 167); Craig Robertson (pages 16, 151, 154, 155, 162, 163 and 169); Lucinda Symons (page 13); Philip Webb (pages 21, 29 and 149).

Home Economists:

Joanna Farrow, Emma Jane Frost, Teresa Goldfinch, Alice Hart, Lucy McKelvie, Kim Morphew, Aya Nishimura, Bridget Sargeson, Kate Trend and Mari Mereid Williams.

Stylists:

Tamzin Ferdinando, Wei Tang, Helen Trent and Fanny Ward.

CHEAP EATS
Budget-Busting Ideas That Won't Break the Bank

FLASH *in the* PAN
Spice Up Your Noodles & Stir-Fries

LET'S *do* BRUNCH
Mouth-Watering Meals to Start Your Day

PARTY FOOD
Delicious Recipes to Get the Party Started